THE POWER OF CULTURE

Dear Tristam,

Sharing with you a copy of my
recent publication, The Power of Culture –
I hope you enjoy it.

Kindest regards,

Al Mayassa bint Hamad bin Khalifa Al

D1429600

Published on behalf of al-Mayassa bint Hamad bin Khalifa Al-Thani
and #QatarCreates by Cultureshock.

© al-Mayassa bint Hamad bin Khalifa Al-Thani 2022

Cultureshock
27b Tradescant Road
London SW8 1XD
www.cultureshockmedia.co.uk

All rights reserved. No part of this publication may be reproduced,
copied or transmitted in any form without permission from the author.

ISBN 978-0-9954546-9-9

Disclaimer: Every effort has been made to ensure that facts and sources
are correct at the time of going to print and that all necessary rights have
been cleared. All texts are personal reflections based on the observations
and experiences of the author. Any inaccuracies or omissions will be
corrected in future editions.

International Distribution
ACC Art Books
Woodbridge
IP12 4SD
www.accartbooks.com

COVER IMAGE: Render of the Art Mill Museum, by Alejandro Aravena
and ELEMENTAL, due to open in 2030.

THE POWER OF CULTURE

al-Mayassa bint Hamad bin Khalifa Al-Thani

Qatar Museums

Established in 2006, Qatar Museums (QM) is the nation's pre-eminent institution for arts and culture. It provides authentic and inspiring cultural experiences through a growing network of museums, heritage sites, festivals, art installations, and programs. QM preserves, restores, and expands the nation's cultural offerings and historical sites, sharing arts and culture from Qatar and the region with the rest of the world, and enriching the lives of citizens, residents, and visitors by bringing international art to Qatar.

Years of Culture

Launched in 2012, after Qatar won the rights to host the World Cup 2022, the "Years of Culture" (YOC) initiative is a cultural diplomacy exchange that deepens understanding between Qatar and other nations. It is a way to introduce Qatar to the world, and the world to Qatar. The festivities last beyond the formal year of cultural programming. In celebration of YOC's 10th anniversary, coinciding with the World Cup, the 2022 Year of Culture will offer programing from the Middle East, North Africa, and South Asia (MENASA).

#QatarCreates

#QatarCreates (QC), launched in 2019, curates, celebrates, and promotes cultural activities within Qatar. Working with partners in museums, film, fashion, hospitality, cultural heritage, performing arts, and the private sector, the platform amplifies the voice of the nation's creative industries. It highlights talent in Qatar, and nurtures the ecosystem for the creative economy to flourish by placing artists in domestic and international art fairs, exhibitions, and platforms. QC runs the Culture Pass and One Pass programs; members receive information on all our cultural programs and those of our partners, as well as priority offers and discounts.

CONTENTS

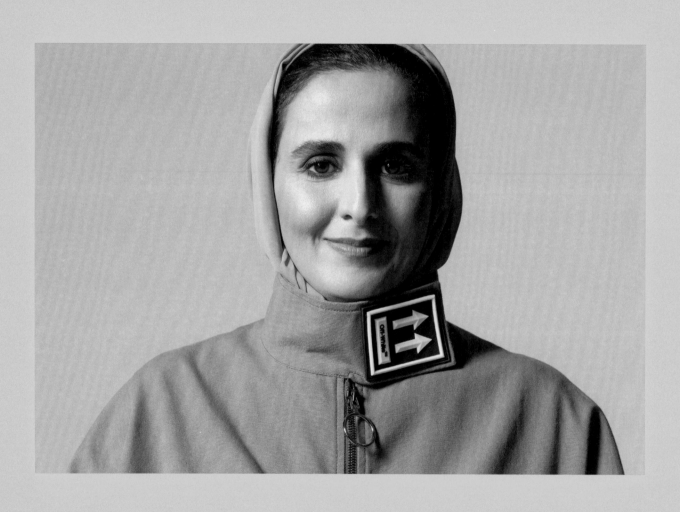

I dedicate this book to my father for inspiring my work ethic and devotion for this country. To my brother for leading Qatar into economic prosperity and diversity. To my mother for being a role model for women and young girls in this region. To my husband, children, siblings, and colleagues for supporting the many roles I have enjoyed and continue to play. To everyone who has participated directly or indirectly to the success of the FIFA World Cup 2022™ Cultural Program and tournament as a whole—the men and women who have worked day and night; we are #bettertogether thanks to you.

The numbers in the circles are
Public Art installations; see pp50–53.

①—⑱

QATAR
UNIVERSITY ㊿

JELAIAH

AL MARKHIYA

MADINAT
KHALIFA

Qatar National
Convention Center

㊼ ㊽ ● ㊼ ●

㉝ ●
⑦

㊿

EDUCATION
CITY

Mathaf: Arab
Museum of
Modern Art ●

Qatar National
Library

Ahmed Bin Ali
Stadium (8km)

㊾

Education
City Stadium

AL MESSILA

AR-RAYYAN

AL SADD

MURAIKH

FEREEJ
AL SOUDAN

ASPIRE
ZONE

3-2-1 Olympic and
Sports Museum

③
Aspire
Park

Al Khalifa
International
Stadium

㊾

8

Lusail Stadium
(2km); Al Bayt
Stadium (40km)

LUSAIL

Lusail Museum
(2029)

72

LEGTAIFIYA

THE
PEARL-QATAR

Arab Postal
Stamps Museum ● 27

KATARA
CULTURAL
VILLAGE

Qatar Auto
Museum ●
(2024)

2

64

Museum
of Illusions ● 5 ● Doha Exhibition and
Convention Center

WEST BAY

Imam Muhammad
bin AbdulWahhab
Mosque ●

51 73

Dadu,
Children's
Museum of
Qatar ●
(2026)

Post Office 68

77

Fire ●
Station

● National Theater

PORT
DOHA

6

Al Bidda
Park

38 58 61 75

62 76

57

Museum of
Islamic Art

31 ● Art Mill Museum (2030)

1 32 33 ●

MIA
Park

● Qasr
Al Hukum

71

RAS ABU ABOUD

Msheireb
Museums

53 SOUQ
WAQIF

National
Museum
of Qatar

● Stadium 974

29 30 M7 ●

78

70

60 67

MSHEIREB 34 — 37 66

39 — 46

● Liwan

AL DOHA
AL JADEEDA

HAMAD
INTERNATIONAL
AIRPORT

8 — 26

AL MANSOURA

AL HILAL

Al Janoub
Stadium (14km)

Al Thumama
■ Stadium

1

#QAT ATES

ARCRE

qacreates.com

REFLECTIONS OF A
PUBLIC SERVANT 24/7/365

Welcome to Qatar. My name is al-Mayassa bint Hamad bin Khalifa Al-Thani. It gives me great pleasure to introduce you to the achievements of Qatar over the past decade, through a compilation of personal reflections. Some of you may be familiar with our museums and initiatives and I hope these stories will give you a global perspective. For those coming to Qatar for the first time, I look forward to sharing recommendations on how to best experience cultural life in the region. Over the following pages, you will learn about our many curatorial programs. In experiencing and engaging with them, I hope you will learn about Qatar's traditions and cultural past, present, and future—and empower yourself with knowledge about the power of culture.

As a proud public servant, working toward supporting Qatar National Vision 2030—our nation's generational plan to transform Qatar's carbon-based economy into a knowledge-based one—I hope you will join me in experiencing not only the joys of the FIFA World Cup 2022™, but also the best my country has to offer. In the work that I have led, my mission has been to globalize the local and localize the global—making sure that as our outlook stays open to the world, we do not lose a sense of who we are, where we came from, and where we ultimately belong.

While the FIFA World Cup 2022™ is taking place, visitors from around the globe will have an opportunity to learn about Qatar, the Gulf region, and the rest of the Arab world. The stadiums are in close proximity to cultural sites, which allows fans to move seamlessly between football and culture. Our ongoing #QatarCreates series of tours, workshops, talks, festivals, and exhibitions seeks to bring people together to celebrate Qatar's cultural scene. In 2022, #QatarCreates encompasses the Year of Culture MENASA program showcasing the cultures of Arabia, Asia, and Africa, and Islamic traditions. Culture is not limited to the notion of art but works as a whole ethos aiming to nurture and embrace all areas of life, from education and sports to business and health. In learning from each other, we create global citizens without jeopardizing our local identities.

Every human is an accumulation of life experiences. We are shaped by the places we have lived, the people we have met, the books we have read, and—fundamentally—the education we have received. Education does not end in the classroom. What we learn from visiting archaeological sites, museums, and cultural centers inspires our imagination beyond textbooks. I was born and raised in Qatar, where I had a relatively ordinary childhood. During the winter my family and I camped and rode camels in the desert, and in summer we went to the beach and went diving in the sea. During the year most of my weekends were spent at the family farm, picking fruits and vegetables, playing with the animals, and riding horses with my siblings. I loved to read and I played a lot of sports. Whenever we traveled, my parents made sure we engaged with the culture of the places we visited. I don't recall when I first learned about my father's day job, but I know that my parents wanted us to have a normal life, motivating us to seek knowledge and be the best versions of ourselves. They both conducted their daily responsibilities with humility and passion and were the best role models I could wish for. Today, all that I am is a testament to them—and I am grateful for all that they have done.

Although people often think of Qatar as a 51-year-old nation—which is when it ceased being a protectorate—it is in fact an ancient territory that was never colonized. It was first identified by name on a map sketched by ancient Alexandrian geographer Ptolemy, who called the country Katara. The land of Katara then appeared in the 15th-century journals and maps of the Portuguese, who described the Qataris as fierce people who could not be conquered. Over centuries, the people of this land—my land—fought for their independence. Most recently, this country's leadership throughout the blockade—when Saudi Arabia, the UAE, Bahrain, and Egypt severed diplomatic relations

#QATARCREATES

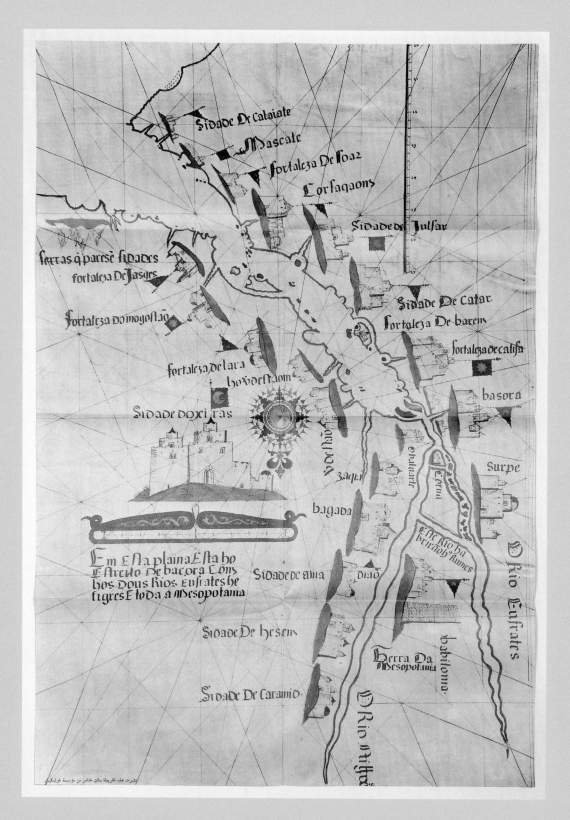

Portuguese map of the Arabian Gulf, 1563.

with Qatar—reflects the nature of our people: proud, united, independent, and true to our Islamic principles of tolerance and self-respect. The past decades have proved that Qatar is a problem-solving nation, a mediator, a promoter of peace and stability in the region, and one of the most progressive Arab countries. For my part, I facilitate dialogue through cultural exchange, aligning myself with the overall vision of my country. I feel very strongly that my father's principles shaped the way in which I navigated the development of our cultural strategy. He taught me to be open to the world, yet true to oneself—and this is the cultural essence of Qatar.

This mission began after I graduated from Duke University in 2005. I started working at my father His Highness the Father Amir Sheikh Hamad bin Khalifa Al Thani's office at the Amiri Diwan of the State of Qatar, and with Sheikh Hamad bin Jassim, then Foreign Minister of Qatar, later Prime Minister. I also had an office at my mother's Qatar Foundation headquarters, participating in Al Jazeera children's channel and the non-profit organization Reach Out to Asia, which provides access to education for the children of those working to create the infrastructure to realize the Qatar National Vision 2030. This is when I learned the normalcy of working seven-day weeks, often traveling through two or three time zones with my father. He set the pace for all of us: his zest for public service and endless energy in contributing to the development of Qatar meant that we all had to keep up, including me.

By 1997, my father had prioritized four pillars: health, education, sports, and culture. Qatar was already developed in each, but he envisioned programs that would stimulate the nation's economy further into the 21st century. He wanted to provide the best education and healthcare systems, and to enhance our lives through major sports and cultural investments. It is hard to separate any of the pillars, so government ministries, private companies, and grassroots organizations all joined to help fulfill my father's aims, which would later form the basis of Qatar's National Vision 2030. In 2013, when there was a peaceful transition of power to my brother, His Highness Sheikh Tamim, my father said: "My heart will always beat with the love of this land and its nation, for it is the first thing I laid my eye upon and it is where my imagination was triggered."

The Qatar Foundation, a non-profit organization promoting education, science, and community development, chaired by my mother Her Highness Sheikha Moza bint Nasser, was established in 1995. Today, a tour of Education City, a project developed by the Qatar Foundation, gives an insight into the cohesiveness of the Qatar National Vision 2030. This neighborhood embraces satellite campuses of eight international universities, the Qatar National Library, the Qur'anic Botanic Garden, Oxygen Park, the Qatar Science & Technology Park, Mathaf: Arab Museum of Modern Art, heritage houses such as the Al Khater house, Al Shaqab stables where Qatar defeated the Ottomans, the Education City mosque, golf course, and the FIFA World Cup 2022™ Stadium. Here, education meets culture and tradition, health, and sports— fundamental pillars that enhance all our lives. The Aspire Zone is nearby, with the Aspire Academy for young athletes, the Aspetar sports medical center, the 3-2-1 Olympic and Sports Museum connected to Al Khalifa International Stadium, and the popular Villaggio Mall, with its Venice-inspired gondola rides. You can begin to appreciate how entire neighborhoods have been established to connect and create communities across diverse nationalities. Urban policies have combined the right ingredients to establish ecosystems that enable economic growth and diversity.

In 2006, Qatar Museums, of which I serve as Chairperson, was officially founded as a government body to oversee the development of the country's museums, exhibition spaces, and archaeological projects. The National Council for the Arts was launched in 1997, chaired by the late Sheikh Saud bin Mohammed

Louise Bourgeois's large-scale sculpture *Maman* looms large in the atrium of Arata Isozaki's National Convention Center in Education City, Doha.

The vast, open interior of the Qatar National Library takes the form of an amphitheater in which visitors are overlooked by an audience of books rising on raking steps.

Al Thani, and ambitious projects were put in place to transform the Arab region into a cultural hub. Major art exhibitions and music festivals were held as a sign of Qatar's new cultural vision. *The Lost Worlds* exhibition attracted visitors to the Sheraton Doha Al Dafna Hall, as did Arab musicians who were brought in to perform in Qatar for the first time. Private collections were bought to assemble what would later become the core of the Museum of Islamic Art, Mathaf, and the National Museum of Qatar's collections.

In 2010, the Doha Film Institute was founded, with Katara Cultural Village officially opening as Doha was named the UNESCO Cultural Capital of the Arab world. A 25-year cultural strategy was drawn up, linking museums to creative hubs, to transform the arts scene into a creative industry. My father approached Japanese architect Arata Isozaki, asking him to actually build his theoretical "City in the Air"—originally proposed for Tokyo—in Qatar to house art and books. At this time, Qatar Foundation was overseeing the building of a central library by the Office for Metropolitan Architecture (OMA), led by Pritzker Architecture Prize-winning Rem Koolhaas. This was planned as an integral element within Education City. We felt that it was unnecessary to have two large libraries, so we made the bold decision to combine the projects, despite foundations being laid and construction almost underway on Isozaki's library. In a digital age—and with a country the size of Qatar—joining forces was more powerful. Today, the National Library of Qatar is a popular destination for all members of the community. The OMA embodied a vision of a 21st-century library that is both functional and timeless.

The Museum of Islamic Art (MIA)—designed by I.M. Pei—was almost complete by the time Qatar Museums was established. We wanted to create a family-friendly institution that would help to build a culture of museum-going, as this would be the first world-class museum in the region. We evolved a plan to rework the adjoining park to add to the visitor experience, including introducing the public to contemporary art through a sculpture by Richard Serra. Engaging with Serra was perhaps one of the most fulfilling experiences of my early career. Not only did he present the idea for his sculpture, *7*, but he also contributed to numerous workshops on the landscaping of the park. Months of work resulted in a beautiful combination of culture and nature, linking the surrounding park to the museum's indoor spaces.

As we were completing MIA and its park, we were also planning the conversion of a former school into Mathaf: Arab Museum of Modern Art. Designed by French architect Jean-François Bodin, Mathaf opened in 2010. It was important to introduce a museum that showcases modern and contemporary art from the Arab world, and both Mathaf and temporary exhibition space Al Riwaq do so. The first shows to be installed at Al Riwaq were *Told Untold Retold*, a collection of stories vividly expressed in artworks by 23 artists with roots in the Arab world, and *Interventions*, featuring new commissions from five artists in Mathaf's collection. Al Riwaq has since hosted many exhibitions, from Takashi Murakami in 2012 and Damien Hirst in 2013, to Luc Tuymans in 2015, and, most recently, Jeff Koons in 2021.

The museum that best embodies the past, present, and future of our country is the National Museum of Qatar (NMoQ), housed in a breathtaking structure designed by French architect Jean Nouvel. It is far more than just a museum: its grounds and buildings serve as a showcase for talented Qatari creatives and entrepreneurs. Wadha Al Hajri, one of Doha's most celebrated fashion designers, has her store WADHA at NMoQ. Wadha displayed her designs at Mathaf before being discovered by the late *Italian Vogue* editor Franca Sozzani. Other entrepreneurs operating on site include Noof Al Marri, a Qatari chef who runs the Desert Rose café; Ghanim Al Sulaiti, a trailblazer in sustainability with his vegan Thalatheen cafe; and Ghanim Al Muftah and his mother, who run Gharissa Ice Cream. Ghanim was born with a rare medical condition and serves

Founded by Wadha Al Hajri, the WADHA label started out as high-end womenswear, but has since evolved to include accessories, fragrances, and a home collection, with a luxurious flagship store at the National Museum of Qatar.

as an inspirational role model for us all—a kind reminder about the importance of resilience in a complicated world.

In the first quarter of 2022, we launched the 3-2-1 Qatar Olympic and Sports Museum. It is the 22nd institution to have joined the Olympic Museum Network and the first of its kind in the region. A legacy project of the 2006 Doha Asian Games, the 3-2-1 Museum offers an inspiring and interactive journey through the history of sport, utilizing state-of-the-art technology. Coinciding with the FIFA World Cup 2022™, the museum will host the *World of Football* exhibition, showcasing the power of sport and emphasizing how we are all connected, despite differences in our nationalities and beliefs.

It is our responsibility to create environments for our children to be nurtured and supported on their own life journeys. In giving them the right references, tools, and skills, we ensure that they become independent navigators of the world without fear of losing their sense of self and wellbeing. My personal mission remains to globalize the local and localize the global for my children, as well as the children of Qatar and the world. The current generation requires us to have open conversations about their hopes and fears. They need to be guided based on today's realities, not those of the past. Each human being will have their journey in this world; we are obliged to live a life of purpose. How we define our purpose depends on our passions and interests: no two people are the same and each of our children should be given the space to grow into their unique selves.

Your visit to Qatar will enable you to experience the authenticity of this country and the results of work by various organizations. This is a hub, one that resonates hospitality, humility, and grace. The population is diverse and welcoming—you will never feel like a stranger among Qatar's community. You will soon discover that our residents are often multigenerational: they originally came with the intention of staying a few years but made Qatar their home. As a mother, I am proud to be able to raise my children with a global perspective yet strong local roots; equally pleased that the infrastructure in Qatar allows for all parents to do the same. Furthermore, the diversity of our population gives children a high level of tolerance and respect for different cultures and lifestyles— something that is becoming increasingly important in a polarized world. It won't be long before you uncover the true essence of my country and fall in love with our cultures and traditions. Life is not about imposing our own values and norms on others. Instead, it's about having an open mind to understand what others represent and appreciate them for that.

If this is your first visit to Doha, I hope you will come again. If you are a returning visitor, I hope you have been impressed by the rapid development of Qatar, a nation that has set its sights on the future, while remaining grounded in our past. In preparation for Qatar hosting the FIFA World Cup 2022™, I have had the most fascinating discussions. To capture the way in which Qatar has stayed true to its local traditions yet connected to the world, I have introduced a podcast with an ongoing series of interviews to complement this book. In hearing about my country through the voices of others, you build a constellation or mosaic of Qatar's faces. Finally, in summarizing all the cultural programs that have been established, and are being organized for this special year and the future, I realized just how much has been accomplished. This book is supported by the #QatarCreates digital platform, constantly updated with events, partners, and exhibition programs. I am forever indebted to everyone working to bring the power of culture to life.

al-Mayassa bint Hamad bin Khalifa Al-Thani
September 29, 2022

The Jeff Koons exhibition, *Lost in America*, held at Al Riwaq from November 2021 to March 2022, featured more than 60 works from the artist's four-decade-long career.

2

CREAT

cultural diplomacy, architecture, public art, and creative hubs

SY

THE

IVE

ECO

STEM

YEARS OF CULTURE

Qatar won the rights to host the FIFA World Cup 2022™ on December 2, 2010. In the months that followed, we at Qatar Museums gave much thought to how best to present Qatar to the world and bring the world to Qatar. One notable result was the Years of Culture. Established in partnership with the Ministry of Foreign Affairs and the Ministry of Culture, these are 12-month-long programs of shared initiatives between ourselves and other nations.

We started in 2012 with the Year of Japan, celebrating 40 years of economic and political relations between our two countries. In 2013, it was the Year of the UK, and in 2014, the Year of Brazil, which was then the venue for the FIFA World Cup™. This was followed by Turkey in 2015, China in 2016, Germany in 2017, and Russia in 2018, again coinciding with a hosting of the FIFA World Cup™. Since then, there has been India in 2019, France in 2020, and the USA in 2021.

These Years of Culture serve as important diplomatic and cultural platforms for international exchange. They present the opportunity for us to work more closely with people from different parts of the world, people who perhaps hold different beliefs, and hopefully in doing so strengthen mutual understanding, and increase respect and tolerance. Although, as the name suggests, culture plays a major role in the programming, the exchanges are not limited to the arts—they also extend to sports, education, business, and more.

The Years of Culture help to reinforce the identity of Qatar. Throughout history our leaders have been friendly with all nations and have often acted as mediators, while, crucially, our foreign policy has remained our own. No one has been able to dictate to Qatar what it can or cannot do, and our decisions have always been based on what was best for the people of Qatar.

The Year of Culture partnerships do not end with the year itself; on the contrary, they lead to deeper connections and the forging of new and lasting networks. For example, in 2022, as part of Fashion Trust Arabia, we are recognizing fashion designers from Turkey, a country we celebrated in 2015. Building on relationships formed in 2012's Year of Japan, as well as recognizing 50 years of bilateral co-operation between our two countries, this fall MIA Park is mounting an outdoor exhibition by Japanese artist Yayoi Kusama, while the Museum of Islamic Art has an exhibition of Raku ceramics—see the Calendar on p154 for more details.

To mark the occasion of the FIFA World Cup 2022™, our Year of Culture celebrates the MENASA region, which comprises the Middle East, North Africa, and South Asia. This includes the countries and communities of Afghanistan, Algeria, Bahrain, Bangladesh, Bhutan, Egypt, India, Iran, Iraq, Jordan, Kuwait, Lebanon, Libya, the Maldives, Morocco, Nepal, Oman, Pakistan, Palestine, Saudi Arabia, Sri Lanka, Sudan, Tunisia, Turkey, the United Arab Emirates, and Yemen. Our choice of partner in this momentous year is a recognition of the fact that Qatar is part of both Asia and Arabia, and has strong ties to North Africa, and this is the first time the FIFA World Cup™ has come to our region. The program was launched in March 2022 at a gala dinner for national leaders and dignitaries representing countries from across the MENASA region, catered by Palestinian chef Sami Tamimi, and with musical performances by Dana Al Fardan, the Qatar Philharmonic Orchestra, and the Doha Jazz Club held in the courtyard of the Fire Station. There have since been Turkish shadow puppet shows and a Manga Style! competition, in which citizens of Qatar were invited to capture the essence of Qatari culture in a style familiar to the Japanese and loved worldwide. The program continues with a great number of exciting exhibitions and events, all of which are listed in the Calendar section of this book.

THE CREATIVE ECOSYSTEM

The Years of Culture are made possible through close collaboration between many different organizations and corporations across Qatar, who come together to make the program happen. Future Years of Culture will include Qatar–Indonesia in 2023, Qatar–Morocco in 2024, possibly Qatar–Canada and Mexico in 2026 to celebrate two of the countries that will be hosting the FIFA World Cup™ that summer, and Qatar–Asia in 2030, as Qatar prepares to host the Doha Asian Games for a second time, in 2030.

Official FIFA World Cup 2022™ poster, designed by Bouthayna Al Muftah.

Qatari artist Bouthayna Al Muftah stands before a piece she created in collaboration with 600-year-old French institution, Aubusson Tapestry. The project is part of celebrations marking the 50th anniversary of the establishment of diplomatic relations between France and Qatar.

ARCHITECTURE

Architecture is the most visible aspect of a nation's character, and also of its rapid growth. When I lived in New York, I would return to Doha every few months, and each time I would notice major changes... new roads, new bridges, new buildings. As we advance into the 21st century, the Qatar National Vision 2030 remains a key text for my country's development. All the new buildings and infrastructure that continue to appear are a reflection of our ambition, as well as a foretaste of what is to come.

Combining the traditional and the modern is a key motif in a lot of Qatar's contemporary architecture. The prime example is Msheireb, Doha's downtown district led by the vision of my mother. Abandoning the idea of urbanization being led by the motor car, this compact neighborhood has been redeveloped with tightly packed groups of buildings separated by narrow alleyways that provide shade, as in old Qatari settlements. The buildings have small windows, thick walls, covered walkways, and *mashrabiya* screens also designed to combat the heat. All conform to the highest standards of energy efficiency and environmental design, achieved through traditional building practices rather than reliance on mechanical forms of cooling. It is a similar story in neighboring Souq Waqif, a place where in the past, people from around the world would meet to trade, standing on boats as the water came right into town. In the late 20th century the souq fell into decline and in 2003, most of it was destroyed in a fire. Instead of replacing it with a mall, my father made the decision to preserve its architectural and historical identity, and had it rebuilt and restored. It is now one of the most popular areas for locals and visitors to find quality spices, carpets, household products, and more.

Each urban center in Qatar, from the capital of Doha to villages in the north of the country, offers different architectural experiences. To showcase this, Qatar Museums and #QatarCreates introduced

Marchitecture, which is a month (March, hence the name) dedicated to celebrating the country's built heritage. Created exclusively for Culture Pass and One Pass members, the annual festival gives access to buildings that are not usually open to the public. For those who aren't around to join in the Marchitecture program, a recent book, *The New Architecture of Qatar* by Philip Jodidio, showcases many of the buildings that the festival explores, as well as illustrating the breadth and depth of the investment Qatar has made in urban planning, and the starry array of internationally acclaimed architects it has collaborated with.

If you are visiting Qatar for the FIFA World Cup 2022™, you will notice that each stadium has a unique architectural character. Al Bayt Stadium, in the city of Al Khor, has a design by Lebanese practice Dar Al Handasah inspired by the *bayt al sha'ar* (tents) of the nomadic people who have eked out a living from Qatar's deserts for millennia. Al Thumama Stadium, designed by Qatari architect Ibrahim M. Jaidah, has a lace-like circular form resembling the *gahfiya* woven cap worn by boys and men of our region. Education City Stadium, conceptualized by Spanish practice Fenwick Iribarren Architects, draws on the rich history of Islamic architecture, blending it with striking modernity. Similarly, Ahmad bin Ali Stadium, in Al Rayyan, has a façade adorned with patterns like the geometric shapes often found in Islamic architecture, their impressive intricacy reflecting the exquisite handicrafts produced in Qatar. Zaha Hadid's Al Janoub Stadium, in Al Wakrah, has graceful lines and flowing curves inspired by traditional dhow boats weaving through the currents of the Gulf. The shape of Foster + Partners' Lusail Stadium is based upon bowls, vessels, and art pieces used across the Middle East for centuries. Stadium 974 represents modern, environmentally conscious Qatar—it is constructed from shipping containers on an easy-to-disassemble modular system, ready to be rebuilt elsewhere.

PUBLIC ART

Public art has always been part of the urban fabric of Qatar. At one time, it tended to be sited at traffic roundabouts. As the road infrastructure changed and roundabouts were removed, we managed to save some of the artworks and reinstalled them at new sites. We now have a dedicated department at Qatar Museums responsible for curating and commissioning public art.

One of our first major commissions of public art was the previously mentioned 7, by Richard Serra, in MIA Park, which was inaugurated in 2011. That piece came about through meetings I had with I.M. Pei and Serra while I was living in New York. Three years later, Serra would create an installation in the desert of Zekreet (see p38), about 80km west of Doha, near the Ras Abrouq white cliffs, which look like Alberto Giacometti sculptures. I have fond memories of visiting this site with Richard and my father. Listening to my father's childhood stories inspired the artist to produce a work that would preserve the prehistoric site where it was to be installed and connect the desert to the sea. Richard spent about 50 days in Qatar and would visit the site every day. He could have gone by helicopter, but instead he and his wife Clara would make the hour-long journey by car because he found it meditative.

Also while I was in New York, the late Roger Mandle, who came to work for Qatar Museums after stepping down as Director of the Rhode Island School of Design, arranged for me to visit the French-American artist Louise Bourgeois at her studio. It was an incredible experience to see her preparing new works on paper from her wheelchair (she was in her late 90s at the time). I was hoping that she might sell us her *Maman*, the last of six bronze castings that were made of her magnificent giant spider. I explained the ambitions of our nation and why I felt it important for her work to be part of what we are doing in Qatar. Louise immediately understood and agreed to allow her creature to make its way to the

Arabian Gulf. Today, the piece looms over the atrium of the Qatar National Convention Center (see p17), which is a busy assembly point for the many delegations that attend conferences in Qatar.

Another landmark commission was Damien Hirst's *The Miraculous Journey*. This went on show briefly in 2013 to coincide with Hirst's *Relics* exhibition at Al Riwaq gallery during the Qatar–UK Year of Culture, before being covered up again for protection during the construction of the neighboring Sidra Medicine hospital for women and children. It was properly unveiled on the hospital's completion in 2017. Another notable work to result from our Years of Culture program is Jeff Koons's *Inflatable Dugong*, a legacy of Qatar–USA 2021. It is a striking piece of art and a reminder that protecting the future of this rare sea mammal is a national priority, highlighted recently in an exhibition at the National Museum.

During the blockade, we used public art to connect with our people and celebrate our community. At this time, a number of works by international, regional, and local artists were installed. Marking the first anniversary of the blockade, British artist Martin Creed's bright LED piece, *1361 (Everything is Going to be Alright)*, was placed on the façade of Al Riwaq gallery, and later reinstalled on the façade of Al Majlis hall at the Sheraton Hotel. Local artist Ghada Al Khater produced a complementary piece, *A Blessing in Disguise*, in neon Arabic lettering, for the front of the Fire Station. Arguably the most popular piece of public art, and one that encapsulated Qatari defiance of the blockade, was the portrait of His Highness Tamim bin Hamad Al Thani by artist Ahmed Al Maadheed. Called *Tamim Al Majid* (*Tamim the Glorious*), it is a street art-style stencil which appeared all over the country, on buildings, in windows, on cars. It became the central image of unity and resistance of the people of Qatar. Public art became a way of communicating our feelings and resistance in the most peaceful way.

THE CREATIVE ECOSYSTEM

Visitors to Qatar do not have to wait long before being exposed to our public art program. QM has so far placed no fewer than 18 pieces of art at Hamad International Airport (HIA)—and one more in the airport's metro station. One of the first sights on arrival is the famous Urs Fischer *Lamp/Bear* (see p40), which welcomes all visitors. Elsewhere, planted around the airport, are a couple of "flying men" by Dia Al Azzawi, a giant wooden "toy" figure by American Pop artist KAWS, golden walls by Rudolf Stingel, and video art by Bill Viola, among others. Anyone in transit through HIA with time to kill can, after checking out all the art, join a special program to visit some of Qatar's museums and other sites. This can be organized via Al Maha Services, which is part of Qatar Airways. At the end of your time here, another of our public art installations may be one of your last glimpses of the country, in the form of Tom Claassen's giant golden *Falcon*, which perches just outside the departures hall. I believe that the more good art is installed in our public spaces, the more people will have a positive outlook on life.

Public art is not restricted to Doha. In the north of Qatar, several major new installations have been inaugurated to tie in with the reopening of the Ain Mohammed heritage site and the expansion of the UNESCO World Heritage Site of Al Zubarah. These include *Slug Turtle* by Brazilian artist Ernesto Neto, and Lebanese-American artist Simone Fattal's *Maqam*. There is also the previously mentioned *East-West/West-East* by Richard Serra, and, most recently, a site-specific artwork in the desert by Olafur Eliasson that continues the artist's long-standing exploration into the role that our perception of the world plays in how we co-produce reality. Olafur talks about this new work in a conversation we had recently, which you can read elsewhere in this book or listen to as a podcast (see p188).

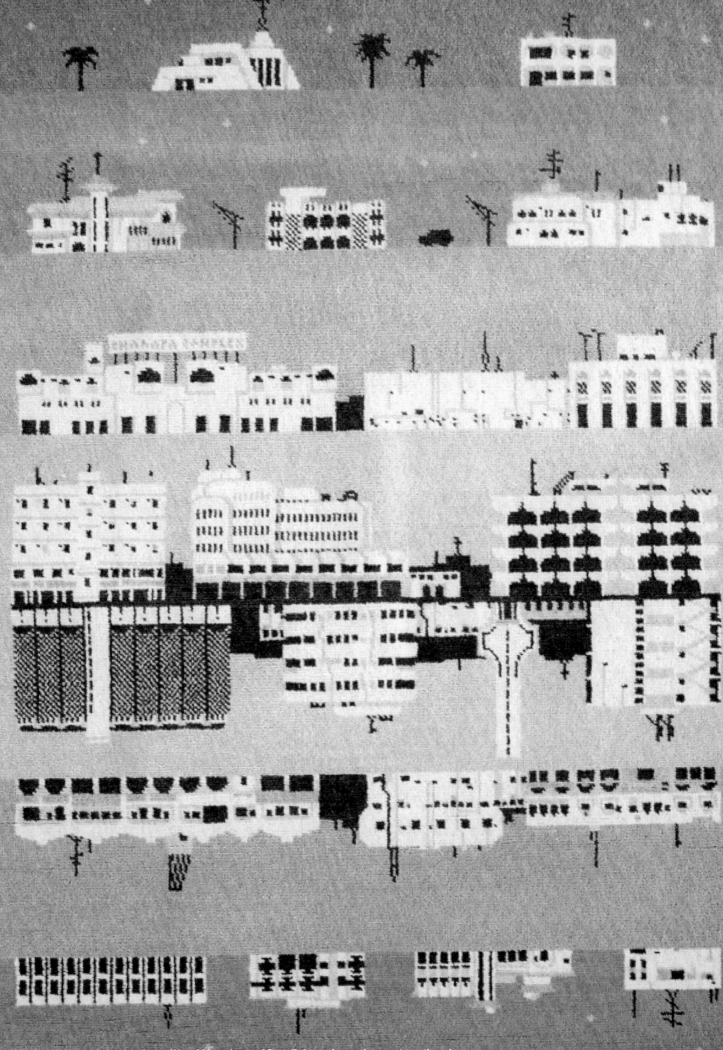

Maryam Al Homaid, the daughter of Yusuf Ahmad, one of Qatari's legendary artists, portrays the urban environment of Qatar on a carpet. Other carpets by Al Homaid portray Doha hangouts and construction sites.

Set in a natural corridor formed by gypsum plateaus, Richard Serra's *East-West/West-East* spans over a kilometer across the peninsula of the Brouq Nature Reserve. The work consists of four weathered-steel plates, which rise from 14.7m to 16.7m above ground, although the tops are level with each other. Despite the great distance between them, all four are visible along the route. The artist has called it "the most fulfilling thing I've ever done". Serra has exhibited in Doha at Al Riwaq and Qatar Museums' Katara Gallery, both in 2014.

It is probably the most photographed object at Doha's Hamad International Airport — a social media post with Urs Fischer's *Lamp/Bear* is the surest way to let everybody know you've either arrived in Qatar, or you are on your travels. Despite its looks, the teddy bear is not made of fur and foam but of cast bronze. This one is the largest of three editions, at 7 meters tall.

The Dutch artist and sculptor Tom Claassen is well known for his depictions of wildlife. He created *Falcon*, an abstract representation of Qatar's national bird, for Hamad International Airport. Taking inspiration from the falcon's soft feathers, the sculpture's curves echo flight paths from Qatar to the rest of the world, while also referencing the folds in the fabric of traditional Qatari attire. The falcon sits on a ledge facing the airport's departures hall. Claassen also sculpted oryxes that are installed inside the airport.

This series of 14 monumental bronze sculptures, called *The Miraculous Journey*, by British artist Damien Hirst chronicles the gestation of a fetus inside a uterus, from conception to birth. It ends with a statue of a 14m-tall anatomically correct baby boy. The extraordinary site-specific work sits in front of the Sidra Medicine hospital for women and children and across from the Weil Cornell Medical School. It is a piece that, since its unveiling, has stimulated much debate, analysis, and reflection.

Rudolf Stingel was born in Merano, Italy, but is now based in New York City. Casting and plating graffiti-covered insulation panels has become one of Stingel's trademark styles. His untitled installation at Hamad International Airport celebrates and honors all the workers who helped build the airport. The signatures and initials of the workers are engraved in the body of the artwork.

One of the most recent public art installations is *Egal*, by the Qatari artist Shouq Al Mana. The *egal* is traditionally worn by Qatari men as a headpiece and is part of their national attire. The gesture of raising the *egal* is a symbol of respect and appreciation toward the country's leadership in numerous fields.

Faraj Daham is a Qatari contemporary artist best known for his mixed media works and sculptures. His art is included in Mathaf's collection. *The Ship* is made of wood and concrete and explores themes of history, place, and people. It adopts the traditional features seen in wooden ships and is inspired by the rock carvings found in the Jebel Al Jassasiya area on the eastern coast of Qatar.

Qatar purchased César Baldaccini's work, *Le Pouce*, many years ago but installed it only in 2019, at Souq Waqif, in celebration of Qatar beating the UAE and Saudi Arabia during the Asian Cup. The big "thumbs up" not only symbolized a sports victory, but the victory of a nation defeating two blockading countries on their own turf.

Sited outside the Doha Exhibition and Convention Center, the giant geometric components of *Smoke*, by American artist Tony Smith, tower over pedestrians and onlookers. The sculpture's powerful form is based on the artist's fascination with geometry and the morphology of organic shapes, such as crystals and honeycombs. The title *Smoke* appealed to Smith because of the complex spaces created within the sculpture, in which its logic disappears... just like smoke.

List of Public Works in Doha, Qatar; 2010–22

This list does not include the 40 or so murals and pieces of street art that visitors will find around Doha and Qatar.

1 *Enchanted East* by Dia Al Azzawi (Iraq)
Location: MIA Park
A carousel with 40 beautifully designed animal "seats" inspired by items in the neighboring Museum of Islamic Art's permanent collection.

2 *Al Sumoud (Withstand)*
by Faisal Al Hajri (Qatar)
Location: 5/6 Park in Onaiza
Commissioned to mark the third anniversary of the blockade, the artwork takes the form of dozens of stainless-steel pillars in a circle with an empty space in the center, where people can meet free of obstacles.

3 *Perceval*
by Sarah Lucas (UK)
Location: Aspire Park
A life-size bronze sculpture of a shire horse pulling a cart with two oversized marrows. The subject matter reflects the artist's fondness for re-examining everyday objects in unusual contexts.

4 *East-West/West-East*
by Richard Serra (USA)
Location: Brouq Nature Reserve
See page 38.

5 *Smoke* by Tony Smith (USA)
Location: Doha Exhibition and Convention Center
See page 49.

6 *A Blessing in Disguise*
by Ghada Al Khater (Qatar)
Location: Fire Station
Displayed on the Fire Station's façade, the neon message serves as a gentle reminder that there is always a silver lining. It references a speech given by His Highness the Amir Sheikh Tamim bin Hamad Al Thani on July 21, 2017, in which he addressed the citizens of Qatar for the first time since the start of the blockade.

7 *Berlin Wall diptych*
Location: Georgetown University Qatar Campus, Education City
An original part of the Berlin Wall, acquired by Qatar Museums as part of the Qatar-Germany Year of Culture 2017. The piece originates from 1975 to 1980.

8 *Portrait of Jean Nouvel*
by Xavier Veilhan (France)
Location: Hamad International Airport
One of a series of architects sculpted in 2009 for Veilhan's exhibition at the Château de Versailles, near Paris.

9 *Turisti* by Maurizio Cattelan (Italy)
Location: Hamad International Airport
A satirical installation of 40 taxidermied white doves, which the artist asks us to compare with human tourists.

10 *Falcon*
by Tom Claassen (Netherlands)
Location: Hamad International Airport
See page 41.

11 *Other Worlds*
by Tom Otterness (USA)
Location: Hamad International Airport
Eight interactive bronze sculptures displayed across three sites. With slides and seats for limbs and playpen-like chambers for torsos, the figures invite visitors to engage with the works.

12 *Untitled* by Rudolf Stingel (Italy)
Location: Hamad International Airport
See page 44.

13 *Crossroads* by Bill Viola (USA)
Location: Hamad International Airport
A video artwork that presents Doha's airport as a meeting point of cultures and peoples. It combines the reality of travelers encountering the work with virtual figures advancing toward the viewer.

14 *Al Koora*
by ROTA Volunteer Program (Qatar)
Location: Hamad International Airport
Reach Out to Asia (ROTA) is a non-profit organization that empowers communities in Asia by providing access to education. This installation comprises 24 paintings representing different elements of Qatar, its people, and its natural environment.

15 *Philosophy* by Anselm Reyle (Germany)
Location: Al Mourjan Lounge, Hamad International Airport
A sculpture created using objects found on the premises of the East German Robotron computer company. The artist's work is typically made with fluorescent colors, discarded objects, and shiny materials such as foil, glitter, and mirrors.

16 *8 Oryxes* by Tom Claassen (Netherlands)
Location: Arrivals, Hamad International Airport
A bronze sculpture of a group of eight life-size similar, yet uniquely shaped and cast, oryx depicting unity through individuality. The oryx is the national animal of Qatar.

17 *Flying Man, Sculpture B*
by Dia Al Azzawi (Iraq)
Location: Arrivals, Hamad International Airport
A sculpture commemorating early attempts of flight in the Muslim world, notably the 9th-century Andalusian pioneers Armen Firman and Abbas ibn Firnas. Both men's attempts were unsuccessful, but they were inspired by the same spirit that would finally send man soaring through the skies.

18 *Mappemonde*
by Adel Abdessemed (Algeria)
Location: Concourse A, Hamad International Airport
A world map using old tin cans collected in Dakar. With this piece, Abdessemed highlights the consequences of the throwaway culture of the modern world.

19 *Arctic Nurseries of El Dorado*
by Marc Quinn (UK)
Location: Departures, Hamad International Airport
A large bronze sculpture depicting a hybrid flower/plant. Although the work is cast in heavy bronze, it is coated with a white pigment, that makes it look like porcelain. The piece represents globalization and the potential to fly flowers in from all over the world in a day.

20 *Desert Horse*
by Ali Hassan (Qatar)
Location: Ground transportation plaza, Hamad International Airport
A calligraphic sculpture that captures the spirit of travel and the flow of movement. The artwork is an interpretation of the iconic desert horse and represents different forms of the Arabic letter N.

21 *Untitled (Lamp/Bear)*
by Urs Fischer (Switzerland)
Location: Departure Hall, Hamad International Airport
See page 40.

22 *A Message of Peace to the World*
by Ahmed Al Bahrani (Iraq)
Location: APM Lounge, Hamad International Airport
A bronze sculpture honoring the work of ROTA, which takes the form of a cube with its surfaces decorated with iconographic elements that stand for the organization's mission.

23 *Cosmos*
by Jean-Michel Othoniel (France)
Location: Concourse E, Hamad International Airport
A monumental sculpture inspired by the oldest Islamic astrolabe in the world, which is in the collection of the Museum of Islamic Art in Doha. Viewed from below, the artwork appears like bright calligraphy drawn in space.

24 *Flying Man, Sculpture A*
by Dia Al Azzawi (Iraq)
Location: Arrivals, Hamad International Airport
A companion piece to *Flying Man, Sculpture B*, raised high on an obelisk-like plinth.

25 *SMALL LIE* by KAWS (USA)
Location: Concourse C, Hamad International Airport
SMALL LIE is one of the American artist KAWS' signature doll-like figurines blown up to giant size. It is executed in afromosia wood; the artist has said that the inspiration for the piece comes from the wooden toys he had as a child. It is the first time one of his works has been installed in an airport.

26 *The Charioteer of Delphi*
Location: Hamad International Airport metro station
Replica of an Ancient Greek bronze statue commissioned to commemorate a victory at the Pythian Games. It was presented to Qatar by the Hellenic Republic as a symbol of the strong ties between Greece and Qatar through art and culture.

27 *Gandhi's Three Monkeys*
by Subodh Gupta (India)
Location: Katara
A homage to India's famous leader of peace, Mahatma Gandhi. Gupta uses steel and worn brass domestic utensils to form a soldier, a terrorist, and a man wearing a gas mask to represent Gandhi's three monkeys, seeing no evil, hearing no evil, speaking no evil.

28 *The Challenge*
by Ahmed Al Bahrani (Iraq)
Location: Lusail Multipurpose Hall
A sculpture commissioned to mark the 24th Men's Handball World Championship, held in Qatar in January 2015. It takes the form of giant hands and arms emerging from the plaza playing ball.

29 *Spooning*
by Subodh Gupta (India)
Location: M7, Msheireb
Two gigantic spoons stacked one on top of the other as you would often find in any cutlery tray.

30 *Rose III*
by Isa Genzken (Germany)
Location: M7, Msheireb
An eight-meter-high sculpture of a single long-stemmed rose in cast aluminum and galvanized steel.

31 *7*
by Richard Serra (USA)
Location: MIA Park
See page 96.

32 *Folded Extracted Personified*
by Liam Gillick (UK)
Location: MIA Park

A large-scale interactive work consisting of 10 sculptural panels. Each faces a different direction and depicts one motif, generally that of a figure. A circular opening in the panels where the figure's head would be encourages visitor interaction.

33 *Bench*
by Saloua Raouda Choucair (Lebanon)
Location: MIA Park
A public sculpture consisting of 17 limestone pieces that form a semicircular seat. The continuous interconnecting stones draw on the generative particle forms of science and the rhythmic, self-reliant structure of Arabic poetry.

34 *Turquoise City*
by Mark Handforth (USA)
Location: Msheireb
A sculpture of truncated turquoise tubes which are irregularly chopped and stacked to form a spiraling structure. It is the artist's vision of the unfolding beginnings of life in recognition of the emerging growth of the Msheireb district.

35 *Untitled (Trench, Shafts, Pit, Tunnel, and Chamber)*
by Bruce Nauman (USA)
Location: Msheireb
A sculpture that is a 1:40 scale model of much larger earthworks. If fully realized, the artwork would far exceed the size of the buildings that surround it.

36 *Allow Me*
by Guillaume Rouseré (France)
Location: Msheireb Metro Station
Allow Me translates into sculptural form an audio recording of a speech delivered by H.H. Sheikh Tamim bin Hamad Al Thani at the opening of the 72nd session of the United Nations General Assembly in New York in 2017. The speech resonated with Rouseré's interest in preserving sound and what sound looks like.

37 *A Family Reunion*
by Abdulaziz Asfar (Qatar)
Location: Msheireb Metro Station
Abdulaziz, also known as TEMSA7 (meaning "crocodile" in Arabic), is an illustrator and cartoonist. *A Family Reunion* is a work of street art that encapsulates Qatari extended family gatherings.

38 *Two Orchids*
by Isa Genzken (Germany)
Location: National Theater
A pair of monumental white orchids created using industrial materials. Despite their scale, the sculpture encapsulates fragility, elegance, and beauty, while functioning as a powerful celebration of life and at the same time suggesting our own mortality.

39 *Motherland*
by Sheikh Hassan bin Mohamed bin Ali Al Thani (Qatar)
Location: National Museum of Qatar
This large-scale sculpture references the *battoulah*, the metallic-looking mask that in past times was traditionally worn by the women of Qatar.

40 *Alfa*
by Jean-Michel Othoniel (France)
Location: National Museum of Qatar
See page 122.

41 *Flag of Glory*
by Ahmed Al Bahrani (Iraq)
Location: National Museum of Qatar
Hands emerge from the ground grasping a Qatari flag. The sculpture embodies the spirit of National Day for all citizens of Qatar, celebrating, honoring, and commemorating the leadership of the nation and its people.

45

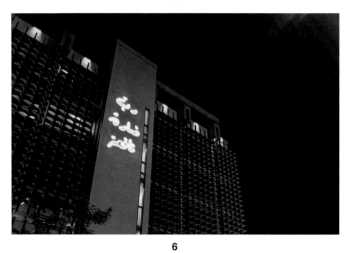

30

27

6

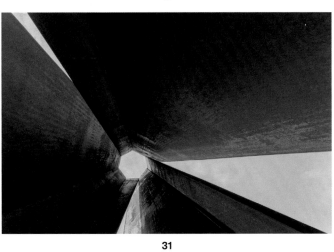

47

34

31

33

THE CREATIVE ECOSYSTEM

In 2020, Qatar Museums launched *Jedariart*, a local mural program. For its first edition, QM commissioned more than 15 artists to paint walls across the city. In 2021, five local artists were sent to the US as part of the Qatar–USA Year of Culture. The same year, QM also held *Pow!Wow!*, an international street art festival, and invited local, regional, and international artists to participate in creating murals outside of Al Sadd metro station.

42 *Al Midkhan*
    by Aisha Al Sowaidi (Qatar)
    Location: National Museum of Qatar
A *midkhan* is designed to distribute scent in more than one direction. This copper installation takes a traditional object for the home and turns it into something contemporary and industrial.

43 *Wisdom of a Nation*
    by Ali Hassan (Qatar)
    Location: National Museum of Qatar
The artist employs calligraphy and the form of the Qatari flag to present an extract from a poem by Sheikh Jassim bin Mohammed bin Thani, founder of Qatar.

44 *Kan Ya Ma Kaan*
    by Bouthayna Al Muftah (Qatar)
    Location: National Museum of Qatar
A conceptual piece centered on Qatari women and their culturally rooted association with *thahab* (gold).

45 *Gates to the Sea*
    by Simone Fattal (Lebanon-USA)
    Location: National Museum of Qatar
A sculptural piece inscribed with petroglyphs found at sites across Qatar, suggesting that the history of Qatar is inseparable from the sea that surrounds it.

46 *On Their Way*
    by Roch Vandromme (France)
    Location: National Museum of Qatar
A bronze grouping of two adult camels and a pair of calves, intended to celebrate the close relationship between Qataris and these majestic animals.

47 *Maman*
    by Louise Bourgeois (France-USA)
    Location: Qatar National Convention Center
    See page 17.

48 *Berlin Wall diptych*
    Location: Qatar National Convention Center
An original part of the Berlin Wall, which was gifted to the state of Qatar as part of the Qatar-Germany Year of Culture 2017.

49 *Sports Ball Galaxy*
    by Daniel Arsham (USA)
    Location: 3-2-1 Olympic and Sports Museum
A collection of sports balls including basketballs, footballs, cricket balls, and more, arranged in the form of a hanging chandelier.

50 *Buscando La Luz IV*
    by Eduardo Chillida (Spain)
    Location: Qatar University
A monolithic iron sculpture rising eight meters from the ground. Large enough for an individual to stand within its structure, it is open on one side and at its top. The totem-like column is directed towards the sky and sunlight.

51 *1361 (Everything is Going to Be Alright)*
    by Martin Creed (UK)
    Location: Sheraton West Bay
This work was first installed at Al Riwaq gallery in the context of the anniversary of the blockade of Qatar. It now adorns the Sheraton hotel, where the bright white neon piece provides visual contrast in an urban setting and acts as a reassuring message for passers-by.

52 *The Miraculous Journey*
    by Damien Hirst (UK)
    Location: Sidra Medicine
    See page 42.

53 *Le Pouce* by César Baldaccini (France)
    Location: Souq Waqif
    See page 48.

54 *Qatari Walls Village of the Sun*
    by Rashid Johnson (USA)
    Location: Sidra roundabout
Four walls embedded with mosaic figures recognizable as human forms but at times verging on disintegration and abstraction. These figures originated from a 2013 exhibition, *Anxious Men*, as a self-portrait and later became a reflection of the viewer.

55 *Maqam I, Maqam II, Maqam III*
    by Simone Fattal (Lebanon-USA)
    Location: Al Zubarah
Three sculptures that can be seen as dunes or tents. Local blue granite was especially selected by the artist for the works to stand out in the naturally pink surroundings, functioning as a sort of geographical landmark.

56 *Shadows Travelling on the Sea of the Day* by Olafur Eliasson (Denmark-Iceland)
    Location: Al Zubarah
Unveiled in fall 2022, Eliasson's latest piece of site-specific art is a meditation on life in the desert. It takes the form of a series of large circular mirrors five meters above the ground via which visitors view themselves on the sandy ground.

57 *Here We Hear*
    by Suki Seokyeong Kang (Korea)
    Location: Corniche Park
Here We Hear is a series of public sculptures allowing spectators to congregate and discuss the past and the present. It seeks to provide a shelter and an open square where individuals, families, and communities can share stories and collectively imagine the future.

58 *Rock on Top of Another Rock*
    by Fischli & Weiss (Switzerland)
    Location: National Theater
Originally constructed for the Norwegian Public Roads Administration then reprised for London's Serpentine Gallery, the work comprises two large granite boulders seemingly balanced one on top of the other. Standing approximately 5.5 meters high, the stones oscillate between stability and instability.

59 *THEY ASKED ME TO CHANGE IT, AND I DID* by Adel Abidin (Iraq)
    Location: Mathaf
Open to interpretation, this neon light artwork carrying the message *THEY ASKED ME TO CHANGE IT, AND I DID* feels like a line of dialogue or part of the artist's conversation with the local community. It is intended as a humorous take on contemporary art as a collaborative process based on compromise.

60 *I Live Under Your Sky Too*
    by Shilpa Gupta (India)
    Location: Stadium 974, Ras Abu Aboud
An LED light installation in the form of an animated sentence in which the artist's handwriting rises and shines from lines of a ruled book in three interwoven languages: Malayalam, English, and Arabic.

61 *Clay Court*
    by Faye Toogood (UK)
    Location: National Theater
An immersive display of 17 giant sculptures hand-shaped in clay-like cement composite, presented as seats, benches, and arches. The arrangement was created specifically for the grounds of the Qatar National Theater.

62 *THE PROMISE*
    by KAWS (USA)
    Location: Al Bidda Park
A painted bronze Pop sculpture depicting a parent carefully passing a globe into the hands of a child. It aims to touch upon themes of family, environmentalism, responsibility, and love.

63 *Slug Turtle*
    by Ernesto Neto (Brazil)
    Location: Al Zubarah
This sculpture has eight football nets facing each other in a ring. Each net represents four nations participating in the FIFA World Cup™, so 32 in total. The center of the ring represents the cosmos. It is a place for meditating on the idea of home.

64 *Zephyr* by Monira Al Qadiri (Kuwait)
    Location: North Beach, West Bay
In prehistoric times much of the Arabian Peninsula lay under water, which is why ancient marine fossils can be found in the soil and mountains in some inland areas. *Zephyr* is a large-scale recreation of a microscopic organism seen in fossilized marine algae discovered on the peninsula, lit up in order to mimic their bioluminescence.

65 *Doha Modern Playground*
    by Shezad Dawood (UK)
    Location: Al Masrah Park
Four structures reference the Qatar National Theatre and Ministry of Information, the Doha Sheraton, Qatar University and Qatar Post Office, all reimagined as a children's playground.

66 *Tawazun*
    by Shua'a Ali (Qatar)
    Location: Msheireb
Constructed from various materials including granite, sandstone, and limestone, *Tawazun* is a pillar that symbolizes the progression of Qatar. The geometric interaction of elements in the sculpture portrays the synergy of difficulty and stability faced in the crisis of the blockade.

67 *Doha Mountains*
    by Ugo Rondinone (Switzerland)
    Location: Ras Abu Aboud beach
Rondinone's "Mountain" sculptures are abstract compositions that consist of rocks painted in different fluorescent colors stacked vertically. The colors of these rocks are those of the Olympic rings.

68 *Algarat* by Mohamed Al Ateeq (Qatar)
    Location: Post Office Park
This installation, opposite Qatar's iconic post office building, is called "Acacia Tree Seed". It is intended to express the duality of human nature, combining the good seed and the bad seed, both inherent in all humans. Yet, the artist maintains, goodness prevails over time.

69 *Al Jassasiya Playground*
    by Salman Al Malek (Qatar)
    Location: Al Dastour
This is a site-specific installation named after the location that inspired it: Al Jassasiya, with its famous petroglyphs. The sculpture reflects one of the markings found: a boat and different-sized paddles.

70 *Milestone*
    by Shua'a Ali (Qatar)
    Location: Grand Hamad Street Plaza
In a series of sculptures inspired by construction debris, the artist explores the relationship between past and present-day Doha. Her work highlights the accelerating development the city has experienced in the past decades.

71 *Us, Her, Him*
    by Najla El Zein (France-Lebanon)
    Location: Flag Plaza
A site-specific public installation composed of a series of benches made from more than 270 meters of hand-sculpted limestone. The installation is intended as an abstract reflection on human interactions, and the sculptures are meant to bring people together.

72 *Egal* by Shouq Al Mana (Qatar)
    Location: Lusail Marina Promenade
    See page 45.

73 *Hahn* by Katharina Fritsch (Germany)
    Location: Sheraton, West Bay
A 4.72-meter-tall fiberglass sculpture of an ultramarine-blue cockerel. The piece formerly perched on an empty plinth in London's Trafalgar Square.

74 *The Ship* by Faraj Daham (Qatar)
    Location: Al Janoub Stadium, Al Wakrah
    See page 46.

75 *Cocoon Earth, Our Goal is the Life*
    by Ernesto Neto (Brazil)
    Location: National Theater
Neto is known for creating installations and sculptures out of stocking-like material and nets that he fills with various objects, or sand, soil, and shells. His work draws from biomorphism and incorporates organic shapes and materials that engage all five senses.

76 *Minaret/Clocktower/Yellow Sculpture*
    Unknown artists
    Location: Al Bidda Park
These sculptures all used to sit at the center of roundabouts in Doha. With the replanning of the road network, the roundabouts disappeared and the sculptures have a new home in the park.

77 *Dugong*
    by Jeff Koons (USA)
    Location: Corniche
Following on from his major exhibition in Doha in 2021, Koons returns with one of his trademark mirror-finish, large-scale sculptures. In this case, it celebrates the rare sea mammals found in Qatar's waters, which were also the subject of a recent National Museum exhibition.

78 *Tob Tob Ya Baher*
    by Salman Al Malek (Qatar)
    Location: Al Najada
This artwork is inspired by an old song from Qatar about "waiting", and was sung by sisters, mothers, wives, and children for their husbands to return from diving, or for their brothers and sons returning from distant ports.

THE CREATIVE ECOSYSTEM

53

CREATIVE HUBS

Investing in public art naturally creates an urban ecosystem for creativity. UN reports estimate that 10% of the world's gross domestic product (GDP) will depend on the creative economy in the future, and the creative industry is a priority focus for the #QatarCreates initiative. We are working closely with the private sector, government funds, and development banks to support the creatives of this country and the region as a whole. The aim is that by supplying inspiration—by opening museums with world-class collections—and by providing spaces in which to develop their talents, we can nurture the artists and designers of tomorrow. I have no doubt in my mind that our creatives are already making an impact globally. In art, design, fashion, film, jewelry, and technology they are engaged in a global creative discourse.

My journey began with the establishment of IN-Q, soon after the opening of the Museum of Islamic Art in 2008. This is the commercial entity that supports designers in producing unique products for the gift shops at Qatar's museums. We started by commissioning for the MIA store. Over time we developed relationships with the artists in residence at the Fire Station (see p62), as well as the Virginia Commonwealth University School of the Arts in Qatar. To date, IN-Q has incubated artists, designers, calligraphers, illustrators, writers, photographers, fashion designers, and chefs. Whenever I need to buy a gift, Qatar Museums' stores are my first stop. The role of IN-Q, under its director Phil Lawrie and following the creative vision of Sheikha Jawaher Al Thani, will become even more significant as we develop our next four museums. For the FIFA World Cup 2022™, special collaborations with a variety of artists and brands will be available in our museum gift shops—notably a series of special World Cup Edition water bottles, led by Olivia Bouzarif, and designed by a host of international artists, including Olafur Eliasson (Denmark), Liam Gillick (UK), Jean-Michel Othoniel (France), KAWS (USA),

Carsten Höller (Belgium), Ernesto Neto (Brazil), Urs Fischer (Switzerland), Takashi Murakami (Japan), and 10 Qatari artists.

In 2010, we established the Doha Film Institute (DFI) to support the film industry. It offers short and long courses on filmmaking, as well as apprenticeships and internships. It is headquartered in the Katara Cultural Village and works very closely with the Qatar University media department and the Northwestern University in Qatar's school of journalism and communications.

Even before its official founding, in 2009 a pre-launch DFI teamed up with Tribeca Enterprises to start the Doha Tribeca Film Festival. It was felt at the time that it was important to experience an international film festival in Doha, and to connect the cities of New York and Doha. The partnership ran until 2012, at which point we decided to prioritize the nurturing of local and regional talent. This resulted in two festivals. The first, Ajyal, launched in 2012, is dedicated to youth. It brings together the young people of Qatar to watch family-friendly films from around the world and vote for those they consider the best. The films screened lean towards current affairs and critical topics, such as climate change, health, and human trafficking. We want our children to think about the world they inhabit.

In 2022, Ajyal celebrates 10 years and, in that time, in addition to the main jury strand, it has developed some specialist programs: Geekdom, curated by Abdullah Al Musallam, is a popular platform for people interested in tech, animation and film, while Ajyali Tunes, led by Dana Al Meer, celebrates music and the human voice, and has just set up a music lab residency at the Fire Station. My personal favorite part of Ajyal is the self-explanatory Made in Qatar program. Some of these films are created by people who have been supported by DFI's second film festival, Qumra. Launched in 2014

THE CREATIVE ECOSYSTEM

for first- and second-time filmmakers from our region, it helps to connect them to top talent in the international film world and mentor them through the process of evolving their own work. Many have gone on to receive international awards.

Qatar owns the Miramax library, and is a major force in the media and entertainment world, with various platforms such as Al Jazeera, with its powerful documentary tradition, and BeIN sports and media. This means that filmmakers who go through the DFI program can put their new-found skills into practice in local work environments. Recently, Qatar has also launched its own Media City and Film Fund to attract more entertainment to our country.

The DFI is led by Fatma Al Remaihi, supported by a talented team. Many of those who began their careers at the Institute have gone on to establish their own companies, such as The Edge, The Film House, and Innovation Studios. When we were curating the collections for the NMoQ, the DFI commissioned films to be screened in the galleries from an array of international directors, including Abderrahmane Sissako, Mira Nair, Peter Webber, and Doug Aitken. These directors were understudied by interns from the DFI, some of whom are now representing Qatar in international festivals with their own work.

In 2015, another major stride forward in the evolution of Qatar's creative economy was taken with the conversion of a former fire station into an artists' space. Called simply the Fire Station, the reconfigured building provides 22 studio spaces for an artists-in-residence program (AIR). In the seven years since launching, many AIR alumni have gained representation by some of Doha's leading commercial galleries, including Anima in West Bay, Al Hosh in Msheireb, Al Markhiya at the Fire Station and the Katara Art Center, Art 27 by W Doha hotel, and the Eiwan Al Gassar Gallery.

Ali H_____assan

Bouthayna Al Mu_____ftah

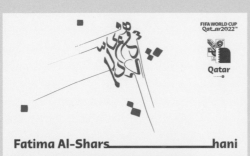

Fatima Al-Shars_____hani

Abdulaziz Yous_____ef

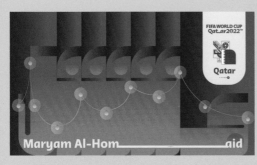

Maryam Al-Hom_____aid

Mohammed Faraj Al-Su_____waidi

Mubarak Al-Tha_____ni

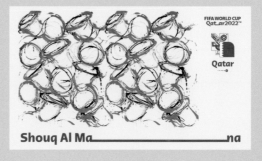

Shouq Al Ma_____na

Noor Abu_____issa

Shua'a A_____li

Labels designed by Qatari artists for Qatar Museums' special edition FIFA World Cup 2022™ water bottles.

A Townhouse room designed by American artist Daniel Arsham. The Townhouses are available to rent and to use for special events. They are connected by a garden and have a common *majlis* where people can meet.

They have also gone to international art fairs and into international museum collections.

In 2021, we launched M7—for fashion, design, and technology—and, in 2022, Liwan design labs. Both are incubators for creatives, offering studio space, business support, and access to communities of like-minded people and entrepreneurial ventures. We are in the process of converting heritage houses in the districts of Al Asmakh and Al Najada into similar creative spaces. Also in the works is the QPS project, a conversion of a historic former school into a vocational school for the creative economy—you can read more about all of these projects in the following pages. Once all these centers are fully operational, Qatar's creatives will have multiple platforms to help them grow and connect with the relevant industries. My ultimate goal is for the private sector to engage with our talented creatives in a fruitful two-way exchange: the creatives receive industry support, while the industries benefit from a flow of exciting, original ideas. A good example is the upcoming opening of the Ned Hotel, a transformation of the former headquarters of the Ministry of Interior.

To see how creative thinking can enhance daily life, one can visit the townhouses that #QatarCreates has sponsored in the Msheireb district. Curated by former editor-in-chief of *ELLE Decor* Whitney Robinson for the Culture Pass Club, the houses make up Qatar's first-of-its-kind private arts members club. The 14 properties are designed by leading international names in art, fashion and interior design, including Diane von Furstenberg, India Mahdavi, Rossana Orlandi, Marie-Anne Oudejans, Daniel Arsham, Chris Wolston with The Future Perfect, and Qataris Wadha Al Hajri and Aisha Al Sowaidi. The houses are connected by a garden, filled with plants that produce the special fragrance "Msheireb", created by the Argentinian perfumer Julian Bedel under his brand Fueguia.

I dedicated this perfume to my mother, as the fragrance of one's mother is always the first experienced by a newborn child. The townhouses also have a common *majlis* (meeting space), where Culture Pass members can meet, and organize and attend public talks related to art and culture.

THE CREATIVE ECOSYSTEM

With my father His Highness Sheikh Hamad bin Khalifa Al Thani
at the National Museum of Qatar.

To connect the various #QatarCreates initiatives, we have created three festival platforms: Tasweer for photography; Design Doha for design innovation; and Rubaiyat, a quadrennial mixture of exhibitions and public art commissions. Tasweer was launched in 2021 using M7 and several heritage houses as its main venues. In March 2023, it will take center stage in a #QatarCreates week of events showcasing new commissions and the regional finalists of the Al Thani photography awards. The next Design Doha and Rubaiyat will both take place in 2024, the former in the spring and the latter in the fall. For further details see the Calendar section.

There are other well-established Qatar festivals, including Katara's Dhow Festival, known in Arabic as *Al Mahamil*, which runs each November and December and celebrates the traditions of pearl diving and the sea. More information on Katara's extensive offering of festivals can be found on its website. There are also a number of special festivals and events planned to coincide with the FIFA World Cup 2022™. These include *Monsoon Wedding*, a musical by Indian director Mira Nair, who is a long-term supporter of Qatar and the DFI; the Festival in Motion, curated by Benjamin Millepied, arguably the best choreographer in contemporary dance; and CR Qatar Fashion United, a celebration of fashion, music and art, created in partnership with Carine Roitfeld, myself and our creative teams. Again, you will find further details in the Calendar section.

The cultural road map for this region is clear: the need to invest in its creative strength not only empowers talented individuals but also supports economic growth, while furthering our aims of converting Qatar's economy into a knowledge-based one.

Fire Station: Artist in Residency Program (est. 2015)

What was once a working fire station next to Al Bidda Park, serving the community from 1982 to 2012, was handed over to Qatar Museums in 2014. We hired Qatari architect Ibrahim M. Jaidah to redesign the interiors while keeping the original honeycomb façade intact. Studio space across the building's five floors is offered to Qatari artists to help them to flourish. It has become the leading contemporary art space supporting creative residencies, with many of those who have taken part in the program gaining international recognition. The Fire Station also runs residency programs in Paris and New York—and more international ones are in the pipeline. There is a wood shop and a fabrication lab, alongside the Fire Station Cinema, Italian bistro Café #999, Cass Art supply shop, space for a music residency, and gallery spaces. During the FIFA World Cup 2022™, the Fire Station celebrates 40 of its alumni from 2015 to 2020 in an exhibition at Masrah Al Maared, a performance space connected to Mathaf.

The Fire Station is also a venue for major exhibitions, which have to date included *Picasso-Giacometti* (2017), *Ai Weiwei: Laundromat* (2018), *Kazimir Malevich: Genius of the Russian Avant-garde* (2019) and *KAWS: HE EATS ALONE* (2019–20). Most recently, from November 2021 to April 2022, the Fire Station hosted *Virgil Abloh: Figures of Speech*, the first museum exhibition in the Middle East devoted to the acclaimed American artist and designer. To coincide with the FIFA World Cup 2022™, there will be a show surveying 25 years of the Qatar-based news and current affairs broadcaster Al Jazeera: see p154 for details.

Reflecting Ai Weiwei's continuing engagement with the global refugee crisis, his monumental *Laundromat* show at the Fire Station in 2018 brought together thousands of articles of clothing collected from a makeshift refugee camp in Idomeni, a small village in northern Greece.

M7: Fashion, Design and Technology (est. 2021)

After the Fire Station launched with its artists-in-residency program, we received many applications from creatives working in fashion and design. We realized they needed a similar structure of their own. At that time, the developers of Msheireb were looking for a tenant for what they had intended to be the district's cultural hub, occupying a prime site at the end of the Baraha, or main plaza. We suggested a center for fashion, design, and technology, something that would complement and not compete with existing cultural hubs. It has turned out to be a perfect fit. In a short space of time, led by Director Maha Al Sulaiti, M7 has become Qatar's epicenter for innovation. Within M7 is Scale 7, a partnership of Qatar Museums and Qatar Development Bank, which aims to assist design entrepreneurs in transforming their ideas into commercially viable businesses. Workinton M7, recently opened by Omar Al Fardan, has a flexible array of workspaces from silent work pods and co-working spaces to meeting rooms and fully equipped multimedia studios.

M7 welcomes visitors with Profiles, a stylish café designed by local architect Maryam Al Abdulla, and operated by herself and her brother. There is also concept store Studio 7, developed by Tariq Al Jaidah and Asma Derouiche, showcasing fashion, jewelry, homeware, and furniture from Qatari and regional designers. The interior space (pictured) is by Seoul-based design lab MOTOElastico and is defined by soft walls, like in a tent, with items presented on metal furniture that hangs from a ceiling grid. There are two pieces of public art in the building: *Spooning* by Indian artist Subodh Gupta, which is two gigantic spoons stacked one on top of the other; and *Rose III* by German artist Isa Genzken, a giant long-stemmed flower rising up through M7's atrium. Additionally, M7 has a number of exhibition spaces: during the FIFA World Cup 2022™, the main space will host *Forever Valentino*, a major show on the Italian luxury fashion house. You can read more about this in the interview with curator Massimiliano Gioni that features later in this book. The Valentino show will be followed, in 2023, by the exhibitions *Vitra's 100 Masterpieces of Furniture Design* and Van Cleef & Arpels L'École's *Around the World in Jewelry*.

Liwan: Design Studios and Labs (est. 2022)

Liwan opened in March 2022 in a renovated building that was formerly Doha's first girls' school, which was founded by pioneering educator Amna Mahmoud Al Jaida, who became its first principal. Liwan's Director is Aisha Al Sowaidi, a successful local designer. Rooms on two levels arrayed around a courtyard provide offices and workspaces for museum, design, and heritage projects, and local craftspeople and artisans. On-site facilities include computer rooms, a variety of labs, a library, break-out lounges, and a vegan café. The intention is that Liwan will evolve into a creative community offering not just affordable space, but the opportunity to benefit from a cross-pollination of ideas and skills. Liwan is on the edge of the heritage areas of Al Asmakh and Al Najada, which have recently been renovated as part of the Ashghal Doha Beautification program. During the FIFA World Cup 2022™, a new public artwork will be installed: *Candy Piece* by Cuban-born Félix González-Torres.

QPS Vocational Design School (phased opening 2023/24)

The Qatar Preparatory School (QPS), also known as the Qatar Secondary School, was one of the oldest in the country, with numerous notable former pupils, including my father, the former Amir. It closed many years ago and is soon to be redeveloped as a vocational school for the creative industries. It is intended that the facilities will embrace traditional crafts such as carpentry, metalworking, pottery, and possibly even glassblowing, but also modern technologies including 3D printing, robotic building, synthetic biology, and digital and parametric design. The curriculum is being shaped by the school's director Thomas Modeen, a Finnish architect and designer. "The idea is to focus on making, and foster learning through making, and thinking through making," says Modeen. Work is due to begin in 2023, with an exhibition opening by Rem Koolhaas, *Countryside*, which will also launch the first vocational program in agriculture and landscape design.

The architectural scheme by Philippe Starck includes a colonnade made of
3D-printed clay columns and 3D-printed clay chimneys for the ventilation system.

The QPS conversion is being undertaken by French industrial architect and designer Philippe Starck, who will be maintaining the essential fabric of the building while looking to inspire its future users. When fully operational, QPS will be able to fulfill the market needs of skilled individuals who do not wish to enter the world of academia. I am a great believer in nurturing talent and passion, and in investing in the development of skills. The future of the creative industry and the diversification of the economy requires a variety of skills, talents, and, most importantly, passion. From make-up artists, to lighting studio designers, to craftsmanship, to painters, and landscape designers—all these people are required to support the growth of the cultural, hospitality and tourism sectors. If one looks to leading economies—such as Germany, Japan, and Scandinavia—50% of their economy depends on a vocational program. The Arab world is full of talented people and resources. It is my hope that the infinite potential of the creative network enables people from across our region to work together and support each other.

Although unused for several decades, the rooms of the QPS still contain furniture and classwork from the weeks before the school closed its doors for the last time.

THE CREATIVE ECOSYSTEM

71

Fashion Trust Arabia (est. 2018)

Fashion Trust Arabia was established in 2018 as a non-profit organization created to provide financial support to emerging designers in the Middle East and North African region and help them step up on to the international stage. Co-founded by Tania Fares and myself—with my mother as its Honorary Chair—each year we work with the private sector to run the FTA Prize, assisted by an advisory board that includes some of the biggest names in the fashion industry. We award prizes in five categories—in 2022, over 1,000 applicants put themselves forward for consideration. Complementing the FTA Prize is FTA Pulse, the first online platform to exclusively highlight Arab creatives. This invaluable resource assists in shining the spotlight on the Arab fashion world's luminaries by bringing attention to the region through features and interviews six times a week. FTA also offers exclusive mentoring sessions with industry leaders. Many previous FTA Prize winners will be presented at the CR Qatar Fashion United event on December 16, 2022—see the Calendar for more details.

My mother Her Highness Sheikha Moza bint Nasser, wearing an *abaya* by Valentino, with Eveningwear winner Mohamed Benchellal at the Fashion Trust Arabia Prize Gala in 2021.

THE CREATIVE ECOSYSTEM

Another local platform I have been proud to be a patron of is Haya, which is where designers of *abayas*—the long robe worn by many Qatari women—exhibit their works. A decade ago, it was very difficult to find local contemporary *abayas*, but today the numbers of designers and styles have made our cultural dress highly fashionable. For example, Belgian fashion designer Diane von Furstenberg wore an *abaya* by Qatari brand Harlienz to the Met Gala in New York. IN-Q has also worked with international brands in the creation of *abayas*, instigating a cross-cultural conversation between very different worlds. It is important to express our gratitude to those who back these initiatives. The FTA Prize, for example, depends fully on the international brands and companies that have been part of this journey from the beginning. Without our sponsors and supporters, the FTA would simply not be possible. For more information on how to help, and who is already part of this creative enterprise, please visit the FTA website.

Barry Diller and Diane von Furstenberg at the 2021 Met Gala.
Von Furstenberg wore an *abaya* designed by Qatari brand Harlienz over her dress.

THE CREATIVE ECOSYSTEM

3

MU

architecture, collections, past and future exhibitions

SE UMS

Museums around the world inspire the creative sectors and nourish local economies. They are knowledge houses and research centers that empower all age groups through educational programs and artistic workshops. Culture can be the bridge that combines art, health, education, and sports. But while museums in many places play a peripheral role in society, in Qatar they are the core of our daily lives and planning. In giving our young children an understanding of culture and a good education, we are securing the growth of our creative sector, which is such an important element in supporting our National Vision 2030. The objective is not only economic diversification but also, and perhaps more importantly, that of enhancing the quality of life in our community.

Our museums are being launched according to our 25-year plan. This can be broken down into three phases: heritage and identity; social development; and global outreach. Our first three museums—the Museum of Islamic Art, Mathaf: Arab Museum of Modern Art, and the National Museum of Qatar—were about what it means to be a Muslim, an Arab, and a Qatari. The second phase, which takes in the recent opening of the 3-2-1 Olympic and Sports Museum and forthcoming Dadu, Children's Museum of Qatar, is about nurturing our people's bodies and young minds. The last phase of our plan is to launch three cultural institutions that firmly link Qatar with the wider world, in the form of the Qatar Auto Museum, planned to open in 2024, the Lusail Museum, which is due to open in 2029, and the Art Mill Museum, which is scheduled to launch in 2030. It is not difficult to construct museums: the challenge lies in finding and harnessing the talents needed to operate and manage them, which is why as well as concrete and steel building we have been investing all along in our people. We hope while you are in Qatar that you are able to enjoy our home-grown museums, and that you will return to experience the grand projects we have planned for the future.

Some of the most significant art collections in the Middle East can be found in
the dynamic settings of the museums and exhibition programs of Qatar.

	2008	**2010**	**2011**	**2013**	**2014**	**2019**
MUSEUMS	Museum of Islamic Art President Sheikh Faisal Al Thani Director Dr Julia Gonnella	Mathaf: Arab Museum of Modern Art President Sheikh Hassan Al Thani Director Zeina Arida				National Museum of Qatar President Mansoor Al Mahmoud Director Sheikha Amna Al Thani
CREATIVE HUBS		Doha Film Institute Director Fatma Al Remaihi QM Gallery Katara Al Riwaq Gallery	MIA Park		Fire Station Artist in Residence Director Khalifa Al Obaidly	Qatar Creates

2020 **2021** **2022** **2024** **2026** **2029** **2030**

3-2-1 Olympic and Sports Museum

President
Sheikh Mohammed bin Abdullah Al Thani

Director
Abdulla Yousef Al Mulla

Qatar Auto Museum

President
Dr Hessa Al Jaber

Director
Alkindi Al Jawabra

Children's Museum of Qatar

President
Dr Mohammed Al Sada

Director
Essa Al Mannai

Lusail Museum

President
Sheikh Abdulla bin Ali Al Thani

Director
Xavier Dectot

Art Mill Museum

President
Sheikha al-Mayassa Al-Thani

Director
Catherine Grenier

Rubaiyat Festival

Artistic Directors
Tom Eccles and Mark Rappolt

Managing Director
Sheikha Alanoud Hamad Al Thani

OnePass

Al Zubarah Visitor Center

Qatar Preparatory School

Director
Tomas Modeen

TASWEER

Photography Festival

Artistic Director
Charlotte Cotton

Director
Khalifa Al Obaidly

Liwan

Liwan Design Studios and Labs

Director
Aisha Al Sowaidi

Design Doha Festival

Director
Glenn Adamson

M7 Creative Hub

Director
Maha Ghanim Al Sulaiti

79

MUSEUM OF ISLAMIC ART
2008

The first of our art institutions to be completed was the Museum of Islamic Art (MIA), which opened in 2008. It celebrates and highlights the greatest artistic and cultural achievements of Islam, not just in Qatar, but across the entire Islamic world. It achieves this by virtue of having the finest collection of Islamic art held in a public institution in the Middle East. Ten years after opening, we renovated the galleries and introduced new installations, including an architectural gallery that tells the story of how MIA came to be and the involvement of architect I.M. Pei in its creation.

MIA showcases Islamic art from three continents, spanning 1,400 years. Our aim is to safeguard the masterpieces in the collection, pass on knowledge, and inspire curiosity about a shared culture and religion that in so many ways are all too often misrepresented. MIA also hosts a program of regularly changing temporary exhibitions. At the opening in 2008, we had a show called *Beyond Boundaries* that celebrated religious diversity within the Arab world. We also installed an exhibition by Indian artist M.F. Husain that was related to the 99 names of Allah: if you look at the palms of your hands, your right palm bears the number 18 in Arabic (١٨), and your left the number 81 (٨١). This adds up to 99—the number of names of Allah.

More recently, we had a well-received exhibition entitled *Syria Matters* that explored the extraordinary cultural heritage of what was once the seat of the Umayyad Caliphate. Using the latest technology, visitors were able to immerse themselves in the historical sites of that country. That over 11 years of civil war have led to the destruction of many of these sites is a crime against humanity. In fall 2022, appropriately, MIA turns to Baghdad, which was the seat of the Islamic caliphate during the Abbasid period that followed the Umayyad. The history of Baghdad is relevant globally, especially since the US-led invasion of Iraq in 2003. It is also particularly relevant to Qatar because many of our heritage villages in the north, such as Murwab, include Abbasid-era ruins. Today, our country is also home to many Iraqi creatives: for example, Ahmed Al Bahrani, who has completed three public art commissions in Doha, including the *Flag of Glory*, a sculpture celebrating Qatari nationhood at the National Museum, and Dia Al Azzawi, who has a Mathaf-sponsored exhibition at Oxford's Ashmolean Museum in December 2022.

Another country with whom we have a historical relationship is Afghanistan. Last year, Qatar led an international evacuation of non-nationals from Afghanistan, and transported Afghans who chose to leave. Qatar was also a hub for transiting people and Afghan refugees. A MIA team conducted numerous workshops with these families and this year an exhibition of the resulting works takes place in MIA Park. There is a link here in that the towering Richard Serra artwork, 7, which stands at the edge of the park, is inspired by the 12th-century Ghazni Minarets in Afghanistan.

Syria, Iraq, Afghanistan, and many more countries from this region are explored further in an exhibition at Al Riwaq gallery, which is also in MIA Park. The show introduces the forthcoming Lusail Museum (see p158) and showcases some of the rarest objects in the Qatar Museums collection relating to what was known as the "Orient". MIA Park, incidentally, is a beautiful family space where the nature and breathtaking views are enhanced by more examples of public art, including a carousel by Dia Al Azzawi and the Saloua Raouda Choucair bench. QM has also recently installed another sculptural bench, this one by fellow Lebanese artist Najla El Zein, which is sited at the heart of our equally new Civic Flag Plaza.

Prominently positioned on its own reclaimed island on the Corniche, the Museum of Islamic Art symbolizes the bridge connecting past and future, with the old city of Doha behind and breathtaking views looking out toward the Doha West Bay skyline.

The collection of the Museum of Islamic Art is housed in one of the most exciting museum constructions of the modern era: a flagship building by Pritzker Prize-winning Chinese-American architect I.M. Pei (1917–2019). Coming out of retirement, I.M. Pei embarked on a six-month journey through the Islamic world studying architectural styles in search of an aesthetic that he thought would be appropriate to the essence and location of the museum. The splendid cream-limestone, five-story building with its imposing angular volumes, and their subtle interplay of light and shade, are all beautiful references to the great legacy of classical Islamic architecture.

The tower that crowns I.M. Pei's Museum of Islamic Art building takes its inspiration from the ablutions fountain in the central court of the 9th-century Mosque of Ibn Tulun in Cairo (pictured left).

The austerity of MIA's exterior contrasts with the rich decorative elements inside. On entering, the visitor is immediately confronted with a stunning, sculptural double grand staircase (pictured). Elsewhere, gently splashing fountains, stone *mashrabiya* (latticework), and the prolific use of geometric patterns all reference the legacy of classical Islamic architecture. Two courtyards, one open to the old dhow port, another enclosed between the temporary exhibitions gallery and the library, offer relaxing places for visitors to reflect and enjoy.

Dr Julia Gonnella is the Director of the Museum of Islamic Art, a position she has held since April 2017. She is an Islamic art historian and an archaeologist, who trained at SOAS in London and the Museum of Islamic Art in Berlin, studied Arabic in Cairo, and worked on excavations at the Citadel in Aleppo prior to coming to Doha.

How do the Islamic collections at Berlin and MIA compare?

JG   They're very different. The Berlin collection is mostly based on archaeology, the Germans digging in various places in the 19th and early 20th centuries, like the English and the French. The objects in MIA were mostly acquired in the 1980s and 1990s from the art market. It is a new collection, largely purchased by H.E. Sheikh Saud Al Thani, then chairman of Qatar's National Council for Culture, Arts, and Heritage, who was tasked by the Amir to lay the foundations for all the country's impressive art collections, including those of MIA. Sheikh Saud was able to put together a truly extraordinary array of masterpieces with incredible speed. His outstanding passion for the arts and his infallible eye resulted in a collection of exceptional quality, which has since continued to expand through major donations and a long-term acquisition strategy. We did an exhibition on him last year.

Did Sheikh Saoud have particular areas of interest?

JG   He was interested in natural history, from dinosaurs to the endangered species of today. He had a farm where he bred, among other things, a particular species of highly endangered parrot, and some pairs were eventually taken to their original home of Brazil and released into the wild. Coming back to MIA, he endowed the museum with a fine carpet collection. We also have very strong sections on early Qur'ans, and on jewelry, especially from India.

MIA recently reopened after a period of closure while the galleries were reorganized—why was that necessary?

JG   The history of the Islamic world is very rich and diverse, as well as complicated. It's like if you were to have a museum of Europe, how would you organize it? Would you have one gallery for France, which has Louis XIV with Matisse? Audience research conducted in 2014 made it clear that the permanent galleries needed to present a stronger storyline to enhance the overall experience and allow visitors to engage at whichever level suited them best. MIA also needed to be more family friendly and to attract younger audiences.

So now we have new thematic galleries and there is a new visitor trail. At the same time, we've made some operational changes, like reorganizing the entrance and creating a new gift shop.

Can you tell us more about the new journey through the museum?

JG   MIA opted to choose a path that places the local perspective at the core of the museum, responding to visitors from Qatar and the Arab world first, then reaching out globally. We decided to start the experience with an introduction to the museum itself, creating a space dedicated to the making of MIA. The journey continues upstairs where visitors find a new arrangement of the permanent galleries, presenting the collection within historical and social frameworks. We try to speak a little more about what is the Qur'an, for instance, and about what keeps Islamic society together, and about education, learning, and knowledge. Although we follow an overall historical timeline, our emphasis is on broad developments without adhering to conventional historical dynastic sequences, which, for many visitors, can be confusing in any case.

MIA's soaring atrium space is topped by a ceiling of magnificent steel *muqarnas* (honeycomb vaulting), inspired by similar stone structures found in the medieval buildings of Cairo and Damascus.

A visit to MIA begins on Level 1, which serves as an introduction, showcasing some of the museum's greatest artifacts, and providing an overview of the topics to come. This is followed on Level 2 by an exploration of the origins and spread of Islam, with galleries devoted to the Qur'an and its history, the *umma* (Muslim community), learning and science, and finally an examination of the rapid political expansion of Islam across the globe. Level 3 takes visitors through the Islamic world from the Mediterranean in the west to the Indian Ocean in the east, and beyond, concentrating on the arts and societies of the 11th to 19th centuries. The main galleries focus on the three "Gunpowder empires": the Ottomans (ruling from Turkey), Safavids (Iran), and Mughals (South Asia). These are followed by displays of Islamic manuscripts and arms and armor, concluding with an exciting new gallery on Southeast Asia, reminding us that the largest Muslim populations reside in this part of the world.

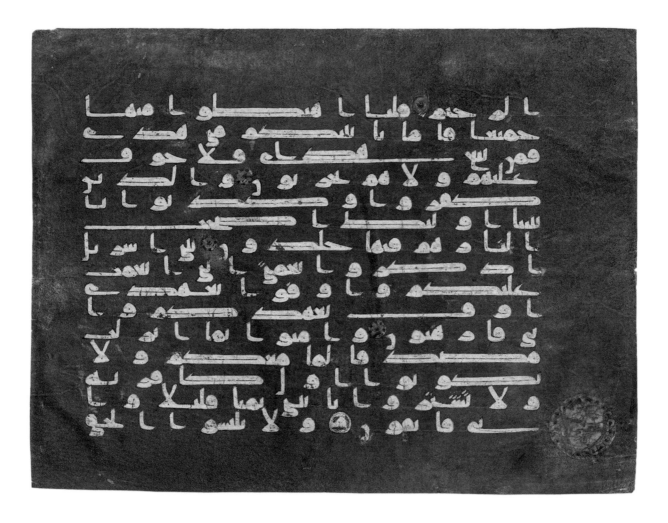

A highlight from MIA's collection is a folio from the so-called Blue Qur'an, probably made in North Africa (or Andalusia) in the 9th or 10th century.

{MUSEUM OF ISLAMIC ART}

Another beautiful object is this Abbasid-era (9th century) earthenware bowl from Basra, with an opaque white glaze and hand-painted blue lettering.

MIA has presented some of the most memorable exhibitions in the Middle East, including *Beyond Boundaries* (2008); *Pearls* (2010); *Ferozkoh: Tradition and Continuity in Afghan Art* (2013); *Hajj* (2013/14); *Marvellous Creatures: Animal Fables in Islamic Art* (2015); *The Hunt: Princely Pursuits in Islamic Lands* (2015/16); *Imperial Threads: Motifs and Artisans from Turkey, Iran, and India* (2017/18); *Syria Matters* (2018/19); *Set in Stone: Gems and Jewels from Royal Indian Courts* (2019/20); and *A Falcon's Eye* (2020/21), which paid tribute to the late Sheikh Saud Al Thani. In fall 2022, MIA presents an exhibition on Baghdad's special legacy to the world. This compares and contrasts the Abbasid city with Baghdad's second "Golden Age" in the 1950s–1970s, when, following the discovery of oil, it became an intellectual, artistic, and architectural capital of the Middle East once again: see p157 for details.

MUSEUMS

An apothecary jar from the Mamluk period (c. 14th century) with text referencing a
hospital in Damascus, which was exhibited in the *Syria Matters* show in 2018/19.

A waistcoat with bird motifs, produced in Central Asia in the 7th-9th century, which
forms part of MIA's Baghdad exhibition in fall 2022.

MIA was never intended to be purely a static exhibition space. Ingrained in its mission has always been the explicit desire to teach and inspire. The museum complex includes a substantial and beautifully designed education wing with its own well-equipped library. MIA's Learning and Outreach Department has run extensive programs ever since it first opened its doors, organizing regular activities for schools and families, including Islamic art classes focusing on techniques such as calligraphy, miniature painting, and paper making. It also offers lecture programs, round-table discussions, film screenings, and concerts and has significantly expanded these activities over the past years as the museum strives to interact closely with the many different communities living in Doha. MIA also includes a gift shop, the MIA Café, and the IDAM restaurant, designed by Philippe Starck, and curated by internationally acclaimed chef Alain Ducasse; the food is a fusion of Islamic world cuisines, meticulously supervised by Sheikha Jawaher Al Thani.

Located in the atrium of the Museum of Islamic Art, the MIA Café offers a spectacular view of Doha's striking West Bay skyline.

The Museum of Islamic Art Park is one of the most beautiful green spaces in Doha. Runners and cyclists can enjoy the 1km crescent pathway around the park. There are cafés and pop-up food trucks, sculptural works by Liam Gillick and Saloua Raouda Choucair, and children's play areas where you can purchase a picnic basket. Regular events include weekend markets, outdoor cinema screenings, kayaking tours, and fitness sessions. Next to the park is Al Riwaq exhibition space and the flour mill complex that is currently undergoing conversion to become the Art Mill Museum of modern and contemporary art. During the FIFA World Cup 2022™, MIA Park is hosting two exhibitions: one on Afghanistan and another on the Japanese artist Yayoi Kusama: see p157 for details.

Standing at the end of the MIA Park pier is 7, an almost 24m-high steel artwork designed by American sculptor Richard Serra. Constructed from seven steel plates arranged in a heptagonal shape, the work celebrates the scientific and spiritual significance of the number seven in Islamic culture.

MATHAF: ARAB MUSEUM
OF MODERN ART
2010

In 2010, Mathaf (Arabic for "museum") became the very first museum dedicated to modern art from the Arab-speaking world. Its opening coincided with Doha's year-long residency as the UNESCO Arab Capital of Culture. Mathaf's foremost objective is to document and archive Arab artists, regardless of their affiliations, schools, and styles, to preserve, honor, and expand their legacies. In doing so, it aims to raise Arab modern artists to the same prominence as their global counterparts. Part of the project is to compile the Mathaf Encyclopedia (www.encyclopedia.mathaf.org. qa), which is a peer-to-peer review of modern and contemporary Arab artists. Gaining a detailed knowledge of these practitioners helps us to shape our own cultural identities, which then allows for dialogues with the wider artistic world. Mathaf is a place for visitors to learn about Arab artists and their work. It is also a venue whose temporary exhibitions, which are both historical and experimental, attract museum directors from around the globe looking to acquire works for their own collections.

The founding principles of Mathaf are underlined by the choice of the museum's location, in Education City. Neighbors include the Qatar Academy Sidra secondary school, the branch universities campus of Qatar Foundation, with whom Qatar Museums works extremely closely, as well as satellites of numerous globally recognized universities. One example of Mathaf's close educational links is Mathaf Voices, an internship program for Virginia Commonwealth University School of the Arts students, in which they have the opportunity to learn about Arab art, hone their research and communication skills, and lead museum tours.

The area around Mathaf is rich in art. The prime example is M.F. Husain's *Seeroo fi al Ardh* (*Travel Through the Earth*), the artist's final public art installation, which is housed in its own building a short walk from Mathaf. It was commissioned by my mother, Her Highness Sheikha Moza bint Nasser, Chairperson of Qatar

Foundation. Indian by birth, M.F. Husain spent his final years in Doha, taking Qatari residency in 2010. Before his death in 2011, he gave his whole collection to Qatar Foundation. This reflects his level of respect for the work that my mother has done, and his trust that we will ensure his legacy lives on. Qatar Foundation is planning to build an M.F. Husain museum.

Directly across from the Qatar National Library (linked to Mathaf by air-conditioned tram) is *The Miraculous Journey* by Damien Hirst (see p42), commissioned and installed outside the Sidra Medicine hospital for women and children to coincide with a retrospective of the artist in Doha in 2013. Adjacent to the hospital, a heritage house, once the palace of Sheikh Abdullah bin Thani Al Thani, a former Amir of Qatar, is now operated by Mohammed Al Khater, an entrepreneur invested in health and healing. It offers traditional and ancient remedies for mothers and babies.

Another piece of public art in the neighborhood is *Hash* ("fragile" in Arabic) by Chinese artist Cai Guo-Qiang, which stands at the entrance of the Qatar Foundation building. In 2011, Mathaf hosted a major exhibition featuring newly commissioned work by Cai, called *Saraab* ("Mirage"). The show opened new dialogues for Qatar with China—in particular, Cai's hometown of Quanzhou —on the subject of Chinese Muslims. This was important as we witness the religious discrimination taking place in China today, as well as in other countries. Here is where culture can play an important and powerful role in bridging divides between people. As a further step in this dialogue, we plan to reinstall a piece from Cai's Mathaf show at Lusail Marina. Called *Homecoming*, it consists of 62 granite boulders representing the tombstones seen in Muslim cemeteries in Quanzhou. Inscribed with one of three different phrases commonly seen on such tombstones, translated into Arabic, the boulders symbolize a homecoming for Muslims who died away from their birthplace.

Mathaf is housed in a former school building, which has been redesigned by French architect Jean-François Bodin. It is entirely appropriate that what was a place of teaching and learning should serve as a museum given Mathaf's commitment to education and scholarship — in addition to two floors of flexible gallery spaces, the institution contains a research library and an education wing. Visitors approach the museum passing by two large granite sculptures, *The Guardian of the Fertile Crescent* by Ismail Fattah and *Al Safina* (*The Ship*) by Adam Henein. The façade of the building has a large screen stretched over scaffolding, not to hide construction work, but for night-time projections of imagery and videos; in fall 2022 it will carry a new commission by Iraqi artist Adel Abidin, a neon artwork entitled *THEY ASKED ME TO CHANGE IT, AND I DID*.

Zeina Arida is an expert in Arab art, culture, and heritage, specializing in photography, archives, and modern and contemporary art. From 2014, she was the Director of Beirut's Sursock Museum; before that she led the Arab Image Foundation, also based in Beirut. She was appointed Director of Mathaf in 2021 and sits on the Art Mill Museum scientific committee.

MUSEUMS

Were you aware of Mathaf in Beirut?

ZA   When Mathaf opened it was a very big buzz for all of us in Beirut. We were very, very excited because it promised to be a pioneering vision for a museum, looking at both contemporary and modern art across a whole region. Its opening exhibition gave the opportunity to many contemporary artists from the region to produce new work. Also, there was the promise of an encyclopedia of Arab art and artists. So I knew Mathaf from the start.

When did you first visit Mathaf?

ZA   I didn't make the opening, but I have a lot of friends [and] artists who were part of the launch exhibition. Then I was invited by Mathaf to give a talk as the director of the Arab Image Foundation. That was my first encounter with Doha and the museum.

How does your past experience relate to the job at Mathaf?

ZA   The Arab Image Foundation is based in Lebanon, but it's a regional project, like Mathaf. We struggle a lot in the region because of political and economic instability—and for many other reasons—and what I was interested in when I was approached for this position at Mathaf was the idea of looking at the long-term vision and making sure we can really contribute to the knowledge and diffusion of the collection, which is one of the most important, if not *the* most important, collections of Arab modern art there is.

How significant do you think is Mathaf's Education City location?

ZA   It presents both a challenge and a great opportunity. A challenge because we're not really visible to passers-by—and we don't have great statement architecture. But it's great to be so close to schools and universities. We need to start reaching out to students and families visiting at weekends to expand our audience. I think we need to do projects outside the museum in other places in Education City, such as the Student Center and National Library. In the coming years we will be looking to partner more with these institutions.

Do you have other plans for what the museum might look like under your direction?

ZA   I would like to bring in more narrative, so that visitors understand the background of the collection, how it was built, who the artists are. I would like them to know about the building—that this used to be a school. I want them to understand the importance of this collection and the role that Qatar has played for some of the artists who took refuge here. And I want them to grasp the stories behind the work. I think that one of the ways of telling these stories would be to introduce a more multidisciplinary approach. For instance, Sheikh Hassan's collection was in three parts: one was modern art, then there were archaeological objects, and the third was his Oriental collection. If you talk to Sheikh Hassan, you realize there was a relationship between these collections—for instance, some of the archaeological objects were in the studios where some artists worked, and he says the objects had an influence on the work. So, I really would like to mix things up as an interesting way of bringing out some of the stories.

What are your favorite pieces at Mathaf?

ZA   It's difficult to pick a [particular] work. Don't forget, only a fraction of the collection is on show at any one time. I would say my favorite works are among those not currently on display. With this in mind, I'm really thinking about ways of displaying more of the collection, perhaps using the ground floor, maybe dividing the building vertically instead of horizontally. At the moment, the temporary exhibitions are given the ground-floor spaces, which are the nicest spaces, and perhaps we need to somehow put the collection at the heart of the museum, maybe even introducing it into the atrium with a small installation. A teaser perhaps that pushes the visitor to really want to continue and see the whole display.

The lobby at Mathaf is overlooked by large-scale portraits of His Highness Sheikh Hamad bin Khalifa Al Thani, and Her Highness Sheikha Moza bint Nasser Al Missned by Chinese artist Yan Pei-Ming.

The core of Mathaf's permanent collection was assembled over three decades by His Excellency Sheikh Hassan bin Mohamed bin Ali Al Thani, a cousin of the Amir. It began with purchases of work by living Qatari artists but gradually expanded to cover modern and contemporary art from the Arab world, the wider Middle East and parts of Africa and Asia that are historically connected to Qatar, such as India. The collection includes paintings, sculptures, works on paper, installations, and video works, produced since the mid-19th century until the present day. There are key works by pioneer Arab artists such as *Baghdadiat* by Iraqi painter and sculptor Jewad Selim (1919–61), and several by renowned Egyptian sculptor Mahmoud Mokhtar (1891–1934). Fellow Egyptians Inji Efflatoun (1924–89) and Gazbia Sirry (1925–2021) are well represented. Other notables include Farid Belkahia (1934–2014), who was one of the foremost modernist artists in Morocco, and Sliman Mansour (b. 1947), one of the most internationally recognized Palestinian artists.

MUSEUMS

One of India's greatest artists, M.F. Husain, took Qatari citizenship after extremists drove him from his homeland. Mathaf holds many of his works, including *Yemen* (2008).

Portrait of a Prisoner (1960) by Inji Efflatoun. The Egyptian artist was incarcerated
as a communist during the regime of President Gamal Abdel Nasser.

Much of Mathaf's ground floor is temporary exhibition space. This allows for some ambitious shows. The museum's first, back in 2011, was called *Sajjil*, a title taken from a line of a poem by Palestinian poet Mahmoud Darwish (1941–2008), who wrote, *Sajjil ana Arabi* ("Record me, I am an Arab"). The exhibition illustrated the depth of Mathaf's collection, with 200 paintings, sculptures and other works representative of the modern art movement in the Arab region. Since then, the museum has hosted numerous shows, including, notably, *Turbulence* (2014) by British-Palestinian artist Mona Hatoum; *Afterwards* (2015), which was a retrospective of work by Iranian-American visual artist Shirin Neshat; and *Cabaret Crusades and Other Stories* (2016) by Egyptian artist Wael Shawky. Coinciding with the FIFA World Cup 2022™, Mathaf will stage several new exhibitions, including works by Qatari-American artist Sophia Al Maria: see p154 for details.

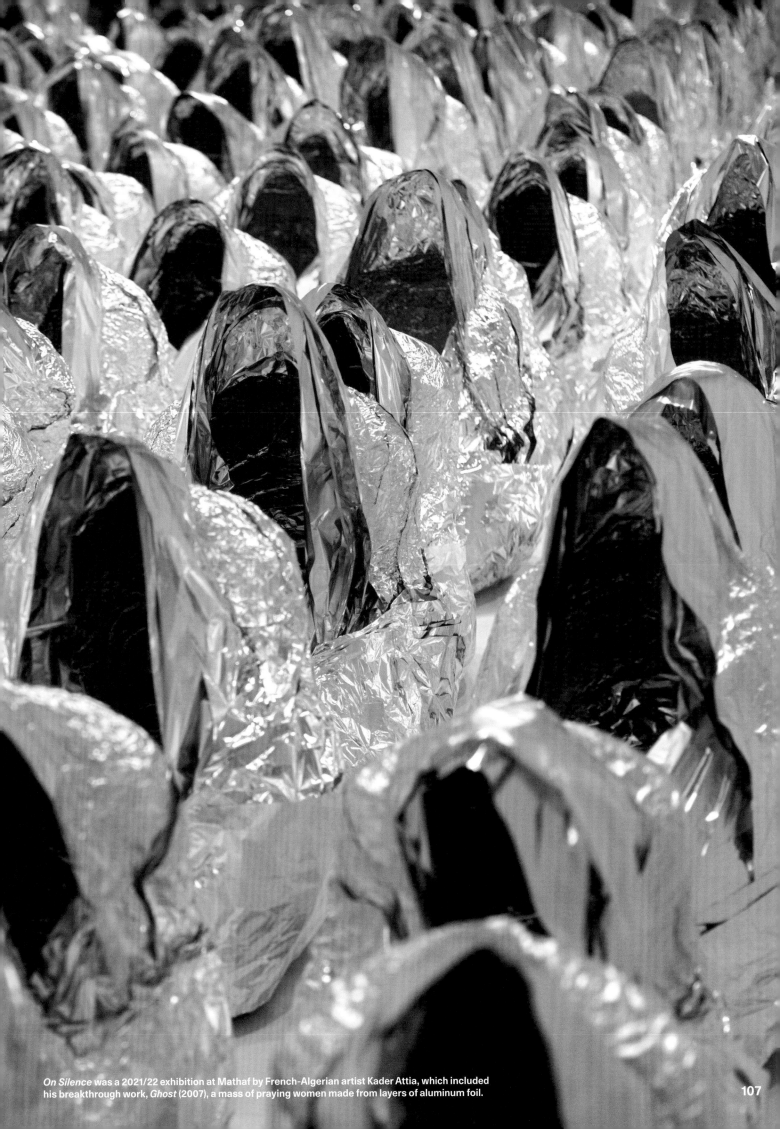

On Silence was a 2021/22 exhibition at Mathaf by French-Algerian artist Kader Attia, which included his breakthrough work, *Ghost* (2007), a mass of praying women made from layers of aluminum foil.

NATIONAL MUSEUM OF QATAR
2019

The National Museum of Qatar (NMoQ) opened its doors in 2019. The vision was of a museum that would present to the world the unique story of Qatar, from prehistory to the present. We wanted a museum that would make all this history accessible in one visit. We wanted it to roam the peninsula, exploring the many towns and villages, as well as the varied landscapes and habitats of desert and sea. And we were determined that although it was packed with history, it should also address the Qatar of today, as well as look ahead. We wanted a museum that embodied the spirit and soul of Qatar, past, present, and future.

This was also our most ambitious project to date in terms of architecture. We eventually arrived at a structure of exceptional design by French architect Jean Nouvel. The inspiration for the building's unusual form is the geological formation of crystal clusters known as a desert rose, which has great significance for desert nomads as it indicates the presence of water. The creation of the museum was highly complex, both in construction and interior planning: Nouvel's architecture presented us with the challenge of galleries with predominantly curved walls. He has said that although the building takes its inspiration from timeless local geology, it represents the audacity and modernity of a country that has progressed at a very rapid pace: "This building could not exist anywhere else."

The story told within the museum begins with the *Qataraspis deprofundis* fish fossil, found in the Dukhan oil field in 1958, and estimated to be 400 million years old. It progresses through galleries illustrating the lives of the Qatari people, tracing their progress from temporary camps a thousand years ago. The narrative shows clearly that movement, particularly seasonal migration between *al barr* (the desert) and *al bahar* (the sea) in search of water, pasture, and trade, has been a fundamental element of the Qatari identity. The harsh environment demanded a strong community bond that was expressed through poetry, songs, and woven *sadu* textiles (the revival of these traditions is part of our creative economy strategy). Later galleries explore the nation's past as a trading and pearling center, with exhibits including some of the finest pearls in the world. The story comes up to date with the discovery of oil and the creation of modern Qatar.

All the galleries are interesting, but my favorites feature the interiors of Qatari homes—I enjoy the detail of the designs, patterns, and objects, and the innovative way in which they are displayed. I am sure these galleries will prompt future generations to create new items for contemporary use inspired by some of the traditional objects on show here.

The jewel of the NMoQ is the Palace of Sheikh Abdullah bin Jassim Al Thani, the son of the founder of Qatar, Sheikh Jassim bin Mohammed, and ruler of Qatar from 1913 to 1949. Conservation work undertaken to return it to its original appearance took several years. The preservation and conservation of old buildings has always been a core component in our national development plans. From as early as the 1950s, we hosted international archaeologists to excavate sites, and today many of the objects they unearthed are displayed in the NMoQ. The restoration of old palaces, such as Sheikh Abdullah's, not only shows the simple lines of our early buildings, but also illustrates how people lived in Qatar before the discovery of oil and gas. We have many more heritage sites around the country that have either been recently renovated, or are in the process of being restored: some of these are described later in this book. All of our heritage sites will eventually connect to create one, over-arching narrative, to which the NMoQ provides the introduction.

MUSEUMS

The NMoQ sits where the land meets the sea, a juncture that has always been of paramount importance to Qataris. It embraces and magnifies the old palace; it speaks of the history of Qatar, and of its land, of its hidden treasures and bright future.

The architect Jean Nouvel forged his reputation with projects in his native France, such as the Institut du Monde Arabe (1987, with Architecture Studio), the Fondation Cartier (1994), and the Musée du Quai Branly (2006). He was working on the Doha Tower in West Bay when he was asked by Sheikh Saud bin Mohammed bin Ali bin Abdullah Al Thani to prepare a proposal for a new National Museum. Nouvel submitted a scheme for an underground museum, but by the time this was presented, Qatar Museums had been established and his plan was rejected. My father then asked the architect to find inspiration from our land and organized helicopter excursions so that he could explore the whole country from above. The result was the concept of creating a "desert rose" on a giant scale.

MUSEUMS

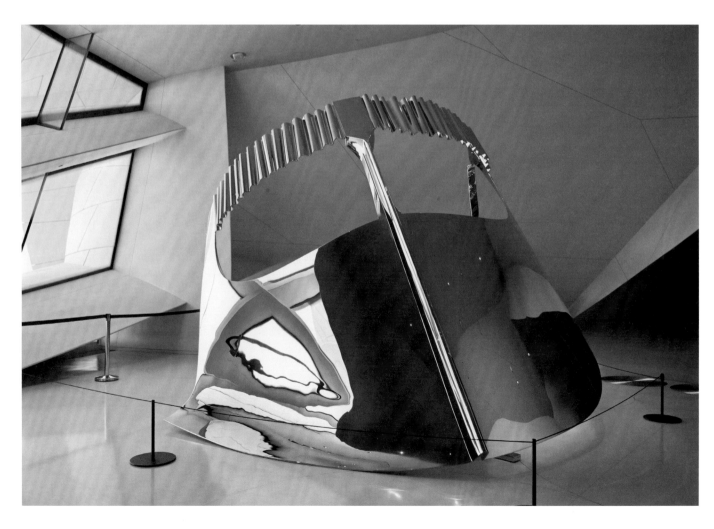

The disk-like formations of the desert rose were re-created on a giant scale with steel skeletons covered in concrete paneling. There are 58 of these disks in total, set at various angles, and ranging in diameter from 20 to 66 meters.

At the heart of the National Museum is the restored Palace of Sheikh Abdullah bin Jassem Al Thani (1880–1957). The disks of Jean Nouvel's building wrap protectively around this historic compound, parts of which date back as far as 1880. At its center is the distinctive two-story Inner Majlis (a *majlis* is a meeting chamber), which at the time of its construction would have been the tallest building in Doha. The palace also included Sheikh Abdullah's home, and those of his sons, and was protected by imposing walls punctured by grand entry gates. The compound was abandoned around 1930 and allowed to fall into disrepair over the next four decades. Following the end of the protectorate, it was decided the buildings should be renovated and brought back into service as the original National Museum of Qatar. This would become the first museum in the Gulf region, when, following three years of research, planning, and reconstruction, it opened in 1975.

The galleries inside the National Museum are fluid and one space is not distinguished from another. This makes for a unified and continuous visitor experience. The story of Qatar is told both thematically and chronologically. The narrative begins more than 700 million years ago as powerful geological forces shape the peninsula. As well as *Qataraspis deprofundis*, a key exhibit is a dugong skeleton, believed to be 20 million years old. Commonly known as sea-cows or sirenians, dugongs are ancient herbivorous mammals, deeply shy and almost extinct. Qatar and Australia are the only places in the world where they can be found. Dugongs were the subject of an exhibition at the museum in 2020. Further displays investigate the region's developing natural history and include models of animals native to Qatar (pictured), from the smallest gerbil up to the oryx and a whale shark.

Gallery 3 looks at the archaeology of Qatar, documenting the arrival of nomadic peoples on the peninsula. The inhabitants of the country moved freely between land and sea, herding and hunting, pearling and trading, as illustrated in the second section of the museum, "Life in Qatar". A highlight is the fabulous Baroda Carpet (pictured opposite), decorated with more than 1.5 million pieces of natural marine pearls, as well rubies, emeralds, sapphires, and diamonds. The peninsula is located at a crossroads of ancient trade routes stretching far to the east and west, and the people had a profound understanding of their environment and a broad range of skills to survive here—knowledge that was passed on and enhanced over generations. Qatari identity is rooted in this unique geography. A final section focuses on Qatar in the charismatic reign of the current Amir, His Highness Sheikh Tamim bin Hamad Al Thani, who continues the work of his father to diversify the nation's economy. This recent history includes the blockade imposed on Qatar from 2017 and ending in 2021.

Sheikha Amna bint Abdulaziz Al Thani is the Director of the National Museum of Qatar, as well as the Acting Deputy CEO of Museums, Collections and Heritage Protection. She leads the museums from macro-level project planning to in-depth operational and strategic planning, including the development of future institutions.

MUSEUMS

What is the vision of the National Museum of Qatar, and what can visitors expect from their visit?

SA   In a nutshell, the National Museum is about identity, it is about heritage, it is about history, it is about the environment, it is about Qatar's connections to the world. The vision of the museum has been to create a space for people—Qataris, but also those coming from other parts of the world—to learn about and engage with this nation's history and the contemporary world around us. The museum has a very broad scope, and with its temporary programing, in particular, aims to reach beyond the country and into the world.

How are the museum and its collections organized?

SA   There are four types of exhibits in the museum. First, there are the archaeological and ethnographic artifacts, as well as the historical objects and archives. These are the core of our collections, and they are the backbone of our stories. Then there are the art films that act as emotive instigators; they don't tell a story in a narrative way, but they are artistic backdrops that bring to life the objects and stories within each gallery. Thirdly, there are models. These are prevalent throughout the earlier galleries, especially the ones with the natural specimens. Finally, the fourth category of exhibits consists of larger-than-life public art installations, both inside and outside the museum building. In each gallery, there is a mixture of these different exhibition elements. However, in all galleries the starting point is the highlight object: this encapsulates the narrative of each gallery and ties its stories together. For example, in the first gallery, the *Qataraspis* is the anchor point because it is the oldest object.

The museum focuses a lot on the environment. Can you talk a little about that?

SA   The environment is at the heart of contemporary debates of global importance, and our museum actively works to promote messages about the protection of the environment and sustainability. In our recent exhibition on dugongs, we partnered with ExxonMobil, as the company shares our desire to help in the preservation of these creatures, and the protection of marine mammals in general. We explained that, in order to protect the dugongs, people need to keep away from them. In a case like this, the role of the National Museum is to raise awareness, then to support local partners that care about the same causes.

It seems there is a lot of emphasis on the global exchange of ideas at the museum.

SA   In the National Museum we explore the theme of our economic and social ties to the wider world in several galleries and through many turning points. For instance, we talk about pearls and the fruits of Qatar's maritime history through a global lens. The aim is to show how Gulf pearls traveled through maritime trade and became a part of many different stories around the world. Then as visitors exit the gallery, they are at another turning point in the history of Qatar, with the crash of the pearling industry, and then again with the commoditization and exportation of oil.

Have you any special plans for the National Museum during the World Cup?

SA   We are going to host an exhibition on nomadic pastoralism, called *On the Move*, in collaboration with institutions from Mongolia, France, Austria, and Sweden, which will also provide an opportunity to showcase some of the Qatar Museums collections that have not been presented to the public before.

Can we expect to see the World Cup be a part of the National Museum's narrative in the future?

SA   Yes, indeed. The World Cup will be documented not only as part of our country's sports history but also as an important historical event, a key turning point in the history of the country. Of course, the 3-2-1 Qatar Olympic and Sports Museum will provide a more in-depth and sports-focused approach as it will fully document the World Cup events. The National Museum, on the other hand, will look at this event not from a sport's perspective alone, but from the stance of its importance for the development and the vision of Qatar for the future.

Visitors at the *Seagrass Tales, Dugong Trails* exhibition, which took place at the National Museum of Qatar in 2021. As well as learning about sea cows' life and environment, visitors were also told what they should do to make sure the dugong does not become extinct.

There are several site-specific artworks at the National Museum. *Alfa*, by French artist Jean-Michel Othoniel, is a series of 114 individual fountains in the lagoon between the building and Corniche that are simultaneously inspired by reeds and calligraphy (pictured). Other works include *Gates to the Sea,* a sculpture by Lebanese-American artist Simone Fattal; *Flag of Glory* by the Iraqi artist Ahmed Al Bahrani, which features the Qatari flag in the grip of sculpted bronze hands; and *On Their Way*, a bronze grouping of camels by French artist Roch Vandromme. Inside the museum are *Motherland* by Sheikh Hassan bin Mohamed bin Ali Al Thani, *Wisdom of a Nation* by Ali Hassan, *Al Midkhan* by Aisha Al Sowaidi, and *Kan Ya Ma Kaan* by Bouthayna Al Muftah, all Qatari artists.

Japanese architect Koichi Takada was responsible for the design of the National Museum's two gift shops. Inspired by a visit to the Dhal Al Misfir (Cave of Light) in central Qatar, where rock formations of gypsum crystals give off a faint phosphorescent glow, his use of soaring, curved and layered wooden strips recalls a desert cave with natural light coming from above. He was also involved in the interior design of the museum's Desert Rose Café and Café 875, both of which are informed by the patterns, colors, and textures of Qatar's desert landscape, and the fourth-floor Jiwan restaurant (operated by Alain Ducasse), where the inspiration is mother-of-pearl.

The remarkable ceiling of the museum's gift shop, designed by Koichi Takada and inspired by Qatari caves.

The NMoQ park is specially designed for families. Its gardens contain only local desert plants — many of which are described in the galleries inside the museum, along with their medicinal uses. There are three different playgrounds: one represents the shipwreck of Rahmah bin Jabir (pictured), a famous Qatari patriot, whose story is, again, told in the museum's galleries; the Dahl is a "cave" for children to play in, which has been designed to replicate the many natural *dahl* that are found across the country; the most recent addition is the Energy Playground, sponsored by Total E&P Qatar, which educates children and families about the development of the energy industry. As a hydrocarbon nation, it is important for our children to learn about this sector through play.

QATAR CREATES '22

3-2-1 QATAR OLYMPIC
AND SPORTS MUSEUM
2022

The 3-2-1 Qatar Olympic and Sports Museum was born out of the love of my father for sports. It was important to him to invest in sport so that the citizens and residents of Qatar might be encouraged to enjoy a healthy lifestyle. I can remember when he was planning the Qatar Tennis Open tournament back in 1993. He was the Crown Prince at the time—and an avid tennis player—and he would visit the site three times a day to make sure the work was going to plan and that everything would be ready on time. It was in a conversation with the former President of the International Olympic Committee (IOC), Juan Antonio Samaranch, during the Doha Asian Games in 2006, that my father raised the possibility of Qatar creating an Olympic Museum. Samaranch told him that no country had ever had such a museum without first hosting the Games. My father's solution was to modify his vision to an "Olympic and Sports Museum".

The 3-2-1 Qatar Olympic and Sports Museum was inaugurated during the 72nd FIFA Congress, which was held in Doha, in March 2022. On this occasion, His Highness Sheikh Tamim bin Hamad Al Thani, Amir of Qatar—and IOC member—celebrated the Qatari athletes who participated in the Tokyo Olympics 2020, and recognized the friendship between Italy's Gianmarco Tamberi and Qatar's Mutaz Essa Barshim, who decided to share the high jump gold medal rather than going for a tiebreaker. The official opening was marked by His Highness hitting an autographed tennis ball with his own racket, used when he won the GCC U16 tennis tournament. My brother was a national champion and, like our father, is a strong supporter of sports, for both men and women. During his time as chairperson of the Doha Asian Games 2006, he gave the instruction that items connected with the tournament and its athletes were to be collected, so initiating the collection that would eventually fill the 3-2-1 Olympic and Sports Museum. His own racket, signed ball, and trophy, are part of that collection.

Situated in the Aspire Zone, which is also a legacy of the Doha Asian Games 2006, the museum includes several galleries that focus on local, regional, and global sports. Its collection is rich and varied, and, crucially, presented in a way that aims to inspire children and families to pursue an active life. International data and statistics show that more and more children from our region—and, indeed, the world—are becoming obese and suffering related illnesses, such as diabetes. It is therefore extremely important to encourage people to be more active and have a healthier lifestyle.

Qatar has hosted many international sports events but has also created a world-class infrastructure to invest in and support future athletes, both amateur and professional. Aspire Academy is the school that produces our top athletes, including the members of our national football team. Aspetar is the sports hospital established to support the needs of local and international athletes. There is also the Hamad Aquatic Centre, used by professionals but also open to the public. These buildings are situated close to one of the most beautiful public parks, Aspire Park, with walking and cycling tracks, as well as the Torch Hotel and a shopping mall. The Aspire Zone project, the design of all of the FIFA World Cup 2022™ stadiums, and the organization of the tournament was led and initiated by my brother H.H. Sheikh Jassim bin Hamad Al Thani.

Each year, Qatar celebrates National Sports Day, a public holiday intended to encourage people from all backgrounds and generations to practice sports with their families, friends, and colleagues. It was introduced as part of Qatar's bid for the 2020 Olympic Games. We did not succeed in that bid, but it remains our ambition that one day, building on the legacy established through hosting the FIFA World Cup 2022™, Qatar will host the Olympics. It is clear to me, and many others, that we are ready. It is no longer a question of if, but of when—and in doing so, my father's initial

MUSEUMS

My brother His Highness Sheikh Tamim bin Hamad Al Thani, Amir of Qatar, hits an autographed tennis ball with his own racket, used when he won the GCC U16 tennis tournament, at the opening of the 3-2-1 Olympic and Sports Museum in March 2022.

vision to bring both the Olympics and the FIFA World Cup™ to his country will have been realized.

Coinciding with the FIFA World Cup 2022™, the 3-2-1 Olympic and Sports Museum is hosting two special exhibitions. *World of Football* celebrates the historic occasion of Qatar hosting the World Cup on behalf of the Arab world. It examines the universal and global appeal of football, focusing on the game's legends, from within and outside the Arab world. *The Road to Doha* follows the long journey to Qatar 2022, beginning with the very first FIFA World Cup™, in Uruguay, in 1930. It brings the story right up to the present, anticipating the final of this year's tournament, to be held at Lusail Stadium on December 18, 2022—Qatar's National Day. Visitors to this exhibition will be able to relive memories of some of the greatest World Cup moments of the past, go behind the scenes of Qatar's successful bid to welcome the world, and gain a preview of some of the future plans for our country.

In the meantime, residents and visitors alike can enjoy another of my father's sporting visions in the form of the extensive network of cycle lanes all across Doha, and also connecting many of the towns across the country. It is possible to get on a bike straight out of the arrivals hall at Hamad International Airport and make your way into the city by keeping to dedicated cycle routes.

MUSEUMS

The 3-2-1 Olympic and Sports Museum is partially housed within the 40,000-capacity Al Khalifa Stadium, built in 1976 and the home of football in Qatar. For the FIFA World Cup 2022™, the stadium has been comprehensively upgraded. Seven matches will be hosted here, culminating in the play-off for third place. Part of the refurbishments included carving out 14,500 square meters of gallery and administration space for the museum. The galleries are entered via a new access building (pictured), a five-story spiral containing a reception area, the Naua restaurant, with its Tom Aikens-curated menu, the 3-2-1 Café and 3-2-1 gift shop, and a members lounge. Designed by Spanish architect Joan Sibina, it sets a fun tone for the visitor with an approach ramp that looks like a running track and rings around the building that glow by night in the Olympic colors.

Abdulla Yousef Al Mulla has more than 35 years' experience working with international and local organizations in sports and event management, media, and public relations, including being a member of the Doha Asian Games 2006 Organizing Committee. Since September 2019 he has been the Director of the 3-2-1 Qatar Olympic and Sports Museum.

What is the idea behind the 3-2-1 Museum?

AM   We have three key aims: to educate, to entertain, and to inspire. We're building a museum culture in Qatar and 3-2-1 is part of this. In every case, we want visitors to come, take a tour, and enjoy the experience. But we want them to come back, because each time they learn something. Entertainment is part of the reason they come back. We want local Qatari people to feel part of the international sporting world and experience the excitement. It starts with the entrance into the galleries, which is designed to feel like you are walking into a big stadium. The visitor is entering a world of aspirations and emotions.

The museum starts with a journey through the history of sport...

AM   Beginning with the ancient Greeks and Romans, then on through Europe, Asia, China, India, Japan, Africa, and the Americas, then into the 19th and early 20th centuries. The museum owns 16,000 objects and we have another 3,000 loans, so altogether we have a collection of 19,000 items, although only a fraction of these are on display at any one time.

How did you get all these?

AM   We bought a lot of them at auction and we received some as donations. Then there are the loans: many of the historic American objects, for instance, are loaned from the Penn Museum in Philadelphia. From the National Football Museum in Manchester we have the ball used in the 1888 English FA Cup Final.

There is a large section devoted to the Olympics...

AM   Yes, the name of our museum is the 3-2-1 Olympic and Sports Museum—the Olympics come first. We have a documentary film we show in the theater that tells the history of the modern Olympics. We have a memorabilia wall and a focus on four Games with a big legacy: the Winter Olympics in Austria in 1976; the 1964 Summer Games in Tokyo; 1984 in Los Angeles; and 1992 in Barcelona. For Qatar, Barcelona is very important because it is when we won our first Olympic medal—Mohamed Suleiman's bronze in the 1,500 meters.

Why is so much significance given to the Olympics?

AM   The Olympics is the essence of sport. Around 206 countries participate, which is amazing. Not everybody can win a medal but friendships are made, between athletes in the Olympic Village, and coaches, and also among spectators. There are great values associated with the Olympics which we feel proud to promote in our museum.

What about sports other than the Olympics in your museum?

AM   In our fourth gallery we've selected 100 athletes from 44 countries representing 32 sports. We have six athletes from Qatar, including Nasser Al Attiyah, a rally driver who also won the bronze medal in shooting at the 2012 Olympics in London—he's multi-talented. We're going to rotate the athletes every three years. At the moment, for example, we have footballer Lionel Messi and his signed shirt, but not Cristiano Ronaldo—at some point this will change.

Among all the items in the museum, do you have a favorite?

AM   I love American football, so I am really pleased with our Super Bowl trophy. I am also very proud of the 1858 football rules from Sheffield F.C., the world's oldest football club—these are unique and were bought by His Highness the Father Amir.

What do you hope will be the legacy from having the FIFA World Cup™ here?

AM   The legacy is already there—in the stadiums. Seven of these have been built specially for the tournament and are going to launch a revolution in sports in Qatar for the next decades. The legacy is also there in all the other infrastructure surrounding the tournament: the highways, the metro, the airport. Everyone appreciates that the government has a long-term vision that is putting us on the right track to 2030, which, by the way, is when we are going to host our next Asian Games. We are also bidding to host football's Asian Cup in 2027, and our target is to bring the Olympics to Qatar for 2036.

A towering wall, featuring all the women who participated in the Doha Arab Games in 2011, photographed by Brigitte Lacombe, welcomes visitors into the 3-2-1 Olympic and Sports Museum.

The museum's galleries start on the top floor by tracing sport's evolution from the spontaneity of early hunting games through to the invention of the rules-based games of today. The story then moves on to all things Olympic. Exhibits include programs, pennants, and quirkier items such as Olympic mascots—from the cute (Barcelona 1992's Cobi) to the perplexing (London 2012's one-eyed Wenlock). A highlight is the dramatically lit gallery displaying every torch from the Summer and Winter Olympics from 1936 onwards, when the torch was first introduced at the Berlin Games.

MUSEUMS

One of the galleries in the history of sport section of the museum, which illustrates
how new technologies expanded competitiveness, with cycles and motorbikes.

The museum's Olympic galleries cover all aspects of the international Games,
from athletic achievements to the design of Olympic torches and mascots.

The museum's "Hall of Athletes" showcases some of the world's greatest sporting stars, including household names such as Usain Bolt and Michael Jordan. Most are represented by autographed items—a baseball bat and ball signed by Babe Ruth; a cricket bat signed by Sachin Tendulkar; shirts worn and signed by Pelé and Roger Federer; the tennis racket Steffi Graf swung at the French Open in 1999, when she beat Monica Seles in the semi-finals; and the gloves worn by Cassius Clay (Muhammad Ali) in his first heavyweight title fight versus Sonny Liston in 1964. The galleries are spacious enough to accommodate life-size artifacts, notably a Formula 1 racing car and the bobsled used by the Jamaican team at the 1988 Winter Olympics in Calgary.

Among the greats celebrated in the "Hall of Athletes" are several Qataris, including
Fares El Bakh, a gold medal-winning weightlifter at Tokyo 2020.

MUSEUMS

Items in the museum's 19,000-piece collection range from signed baseballs up to the
Formula 1 car driven by Michael Schumacher in his title-winning 2000 season.

The final section of the museum is the Activation Zone, which is where the fun is really ramped up. Visitors collect a wristband before going on to play 18 interactive games. Each of these is designed to test physical abilities. For example, there is a cycling game to test stamina and a paddle board simulation to determine balance. Other games measure hand-eye coordination, strength, reactions, decision-making, and the participant's ability to work in a team. At the end, visitors swipe their wristbands at a kiosk to collect an individualized profile. In addition, the read-out compares scores with those of other museum-goers of the same age and suggests what sports that person might excel at. It even links to an app that makes recommendations for local clubs, coaches, and facilities offering those activities.

The 3-2-1 Qatar Olympic and Sports Museum hosts several special works of art. These include a piece by Takashi Murakami, commissioned to celebrate 50 years of diplomatic relations between Qatar and Japan. There are works by Andy Warhol and Jean-Michel Basquiat, and a site-specific installation by Daniel Arsham, which is made up of all the balls used in sports around the world (pictured). This last project was commissioned as part of the Qatar–USA Year of Culture 2021 program. Recently, a dynamic large-scale sculpture of French football hero Zinedine Zidane by Algerian-born French artist Adel Abdessemed has been installed outside the museum. Coinciding with the FIFA World Cup 2022™, the museum will be screening Douglas Gordon and Philippe Parreno's *Zidane, a 21st Century Portrait*, which follows the French soccer star in real time over the course of a single match. In 2023, these works will be joined by a new piece from Indian artist Jitish Kallat.

143

FUTURE MUSEUMS
2023–2030

Qatar Museums has plans for four further institutions to complete our Qatar National Vision 2030 goals. Dadu, Children's Museum of Qatar will focus on play and learning for children. The Qatar Auto Museum will celebrate a unique partnership between the private and public sectors, involving all the families that set up the country's founding car dealerships. We launched this project at the National Museum of Qatar in 2022 and, in advance of its opening, plan a larger exhibition in the fall of 2023. This will be curated in collaboration with Rem Koolhaas's OMA, the official architects of the Qatar Auto Museum. The institution will support our investments in the automotive industry, and enhance our appeal as a host for global auto events, which currently already include the Qatar Geneva International Motor Show, the MotoGP Grand Prix of Qatar, and Formula 1.

The Lusail Museum will house the largest collection of Orientalist paintings and photography in the world. Acting as a central think-tank, partnering with other museums, research institutions, governments and universities around the world, and furthering discourse on the state of the Arab world today, it will align with Qatar's long-standing foreign policy of empowering the voices of Arabs and standing up for their values. During the FIFA World Cup 2022™, this message will be amplified by four exhibitions: one on Palestine, another on Afghanistan, a third celebrating 25 years of Al Jazeera, and the fourth, *Raku*, combining Japanese ceramics with the poetry of the nation's founder Sheikh Jassim bin Mohammed —see the Exhibitions Calendar section for dates and locations. Recently, Qatar Museums facilitated a partnership between Bard College in Ramallah and Education Above All, a charity founded by my mother that aims to ensure inclusive and equitable quality education for vulnerable and marginalized people, especially in the developing world, as an enabler of human development. It is my hope that the participating scholarship students will harness the power of art to promote social justice for all.

The final chapter in our museum plan is the Art Mill Museum, which will occupy a former flour mill on a waterfront site close to the Museum of Islamic Art. It will house an international collection of modern and contemporary art in all its forms. The museum will be supported by a creative village that will encourage the growth of the creative ecosystem we are developing. There is more information about this exciting quartet of new ventures in the pages that follow.

Fifteen years of our quarter-century program have now been successfully implemented. I hope that Qatar's citizens and visitors have benefited from an enhancement in the quality of their lives. As you can see, plans for the next decade are well in place, and we will continue to build on the successes of this family of museums. As we prepare our future museums, we are busy engaging the public with various workshops and exhibitions, letting everybody know what is coming up. Studies have shown that museums are not only centers of knowledge, they improve the quality of our lives by providing inspiration and new experiences. They can even be healing centers for the young, disabled, and elderly. They offer us the opportunity to connect with like-minded people, and also travel inward and examine our own responses to the questions they pose.

MUSEUMS

Dadu, Children's Museum of Qatar (planned for 2026)

Dadu is an old Arabic word relating to play and is also the name of Qatar's new children's museum. Sited in Al Bidda Park, which has long been a destination for families, its aim is to introduce young people to the core values at the heart of the national vision for Qatar. These are translated into four galleries: gallery one is about literacy, life-long learning, and creative skills; gallery two focuses on health and emotional wellness, confidence-building, motivation, and leadership; gallery three is about valuing the environment and sustainability; and gallery four deals with heritage, culture, family, and global citizenship. Each includes an array of fun learning activities for age groups one to three, four to seven, and eight to 11. But there is also plenty to keep moms, dads, and other guardian adults involved—after all, everyone is a child at heart. The museum gardens open in fall 2022, when they will play host to a range of activities coinciding with the FIFA World Cup 2022. Adjacent to Dadu is the Agrite Expo innovation center, which, in the future, will be converted into a school in the daytime, and a teacher and teenage hub after hours.

MUSEUMS

Dadu has been designed by Netherlands architect Ben van Berkel. Its structure
represents the blocks of knowledge, scattered as though they have been played with.

Qatar Auto Museum (planned for 2024)

With the Qatar Auto Museum, QM is creating a magnet for car lovers, design enthusiasts — and possibly even environmentalists. Under the supervision of architect Rem Koolhaas and his OMA practice, and utilizing the setting of a former convention and conference center near the Katara Cultural Village, the new museum will contain galleries for both permanent and temporary exhibitions that will explore the past, present, and future of the automobile, and its impact on life and culture (including as a facilitator of our country's growth). As well as tracing the history of auto development, it will examine the engineering and design processes being developed today in a bid to create greener vehicles. The museum is being brought about through partnerships between the private sector, car collectors, research institutions, and universities, such as Qatar University and Texas A&M Qatar. The Qatar Auto Museum advisory board is chaired by Dr. Hessa Al Jaber, who is also a Supervisory Board Member of Volkswagen.

In honor of the museum to come, *A Sneak Peek at Qatar Auto Museum* is an exhibition featuring three spectacular cars in the Mawater Gallery at the National Museum of Qatar, on view until January 20, 2023.

MUSEUMS

Lusail Museum (planned for 2028/29)

Lusail is a new city district on the northern edge of Doha with a waterfront promenade, marina, shopping malls, business districts, its own tram line, and a new 80,000-capacity stadium designed by British firm Foster + Partners, which is one of the FIFA World Cup 2022™ venues. The Lusail Museum will house an extensive collection of Orientalist paintings, drawings, and photography. While the exhibits tend to depict the Orient through the gaze of Western artists, the museum will aim to redirect this gaze toward the East. Collections will also include documentation of the history of the broadcaster Al Jazeera and the Doha Film Institute archives of films produced by Arab filmmakers. The institution will seek to spark conversations about decolonization, multiple representation, and tolerance and peace. The building is being designed by the Swiss architectural practice Herzog & de Meuron, best known for London's Tate Modern. Construction begins in 2023, which, coincidentally, marks the 50th anniversary of Qatar–Swiss diplomatic relations.

The exterior shape of the building and interior space are defined by spheres. The museum will have four "anchor" spaces — soaring rooms inspired by domes from Egypt, Iran, Spain, and Turkey.

MUSEUMS

The new museum will sit on Al Maha Island, which it will share with the Lusail Wonderland funfair. The museum will offer visitors guided tours of the nearby fort and restored houses of the founder of Qatar, Sheikh Jassim bin Mohammed.

Art Mill Museum (planned for 2030)

The Art Mill Museum will display modern and contemporary art from 1830 to the present, drawn from a collection that has been assembled over the past 40 years. It will include icons of visual art in all media, architecture and design, films and film props, fashion, craft, and more, representing all regions of the globe on an equal basis. The building, which is a conversion of an old flour mill, is being designed by Pritzker Prize-winning Chilean architect Alejandro Aravena and his ELEMENTAL studio. From October 2022, the site is being celebrated through commissions from five artists, all of whom will offer pieces responding to the former mill. In addition, an exhibition on the future gardens that will surround the museum is on view at Al Najada Heritage House #15.

MUSEUMS

By 2024, a James Corner-designed park will connect the site of the Art Mill Museum
with the National Museum of Qatar via a bridge for pedestrians, runners, and cyclists.

Civic Flag Plaza (2022)

The inauguration of the Civic Flag Plaza alongside the reopening of the Museum of Islamic Art, and in time for the FIFA 2022 World Cup, is both symbolic and significant. Symbolic as the FIFA World Cup™ is all about flags — and significant because it includes all the nations with embassies in Qatar, meaning that football fans from around the world visiting to watch the tournament will be made to feel welcome, even if their own country is not participating. The plaza is part of the new James Corner-designed park that will connect the two sides of the Corniche (which currently separates the National Museum and Museum of Islamic Art) with a pedestrian bridge, enhance access to museums and Doha Port with underground parking, and provide space for new art installations and children's playgrounds.

The new Civic Flag Plaza embraces all the countries that have an embassy in Qatar. It is the welcoming face of Doha's cultural district, where all communities can gather to celebrate their traditions.

MUSEUMS

Other museums

Not all of the country's museums are developed and managed by Qatar Museums. There are others that are privately managed, and which also offer interesting experiences for residents and visitors alike. The Msheireb Museums are great examples of restored and repurposed heritage houses converted into public museums, well situated in a district that is one of the most innovative architectural destinations in Qatar.

ARAB POSTAL STAMP MUSEUM

Katara Cultural Village
Founded in 2010, the Arab Postal Stamp Museum holds a multi-themed stamp collection which covers 22 Arab countries. The museum was recently part of the cultural festival organized to coincide with Doha's term as Capital of Arab Culture. It is housed in an attractive building within the Katara Cultural Village, which has many other enjoyable things to see and do.

MSHEIREB MUSEUMS

Msheireb Museums occupy four sensitively renovated, single-story historic heritage houses adjacent to each other in the heart of the Msheireb district. They form an important part of Qatar's national history and reveal unique aspects of the nation's cultural and social development.

Bin Jelmood House
The aim of Bin Jelmood House is to raise awareness and play a pivotal role in the global abolition of human exploitation. The house tells of a time when there was a flourishing trade in enslaved people around the Indian Ocean, a vast region of which the countries of the Arabian Gulf are a part. It also showcases and pays tribute to human perseverance and acknowledges the cumulative social, cultural, and economic contribution of formerly enslaved people to the development of human civilizations.

Company House
Set within a house that was once used as the headquarters for Qatar's first oil company, this museum tells the story of the pioneering Qatari petroleum industry workers and their families, who helped transform Qatar into a modern society. It provides first-hand accounts of the men who labored not just to provide for their families but also to lay the foundations for their emerging nation.

Mohammed Bin Jassim House
In this heritage house visitors travel back in time to gain an appreciation of Doha's history and unique architectural heritage. Built by Sheikh Mohammed Bin Jassim Al Thani, son of the founder of modern Qatar, it documents the transformation of Msheireb over time, recalling memories of the district's past, showcasing its present, and engaging visitors in the plans for the future. The museum houses the Echo Memory Art Project using objects uncovered during excavation work on the site.

Radwani House
Built in the 1920s, this restored house is located between Al-Jasrah and Msheireb, two of Doha's oldest quarters. It gathers, preserves, and shares memories, giving visitors an insight into how family life has evolved in Qatar.

MUSEUM OF ILLUSIONS

Gate Mall, Doha Exhibition and Convention Center
Not so much a museum as a visual playground of holograms, tricks on perception, and optical art installations. Along with the play, there are lessons in science, mathematics and the workings of the human brain. It is an intriguing and fun experience for all ages, ideal for family and group visits. Multilingual guides are on hand to help show visitors around.

QASR AL HUKUM

This is an exclusive and newly developed bespoke museum located in the Old Doha Palace of the Amiri Diwan, which is the seat of government of the State of Qatar. The museum offers an insight into the history of the State of Qatar and a glimpse into the historical seat of governance. Located at the heart of Msheireb, adjacent to the Corniche, and just a few kilometers from the National Museum of Qatar, the museum unfolds through a trail that takes in a series of stops in the two courtyards of the Old Palace. Visitors have the chance to find out about the history of Al Bidda Fort, the palace's architecture, and the urban planning around it. There are first-hand accounts of the early days of Qatar and how it was to work with its leaders. In a room dedicated to governance and international relations there are personal belongings of the leaders of the country and a selection of diplomatic gifts. Visitors may also access the official majlis and banquet room. In the "Experiences gallery" interactive displays allow an exploration of the symbols of the nation, such as the story of the flag, the national anthem, and National Day. A tour culminates in an immersive film that brings to life the story of the people and the land. Visits must be booked in advance on the Amiri Diwan website.

SHEIKH FAISAL BIN QASSIM AL THANI MUSEUM

Al Samriya, 40km from Doha
Away from the capital is the imposing stone palace that houses the Sheikh Faisal Bin Qassim Al Thani Museum (FBQ Museum for short), one of the world's largest private museums. It tells the story of Qatar through the lens of one of its richest entrepreneurs. The eclectic holdings range from the Jurassic to the present day, with a priceless art collection, and an array of international artifacts the Sheikh has collected on his travels. Exhibits include a traditional Syrian home brought in from Damascus and reconstructed on site, complete with a courtyard and two living spaces; a Qur'an room, which also has an example of a *kiswa*, the cloth which covers the Ka'aba, Islam's holiest site; over 700 carpets; and more than 600 vehicles, featuring everything from steam cars to convertibles.

MAL LAWAL EXHIBITION PARTICIPANTS

Mal Lawal ("of the past") is an exhibition organized by the National Museum of Qatar that explores the practice of collecting in Qatar and the Gulf region. Below are three examples of private museums, now open to the public, that are owned by collectors taking part.

SALEM SAEED AL MOHANNADI CAR MUSEUM

Al Shammal Municipality
Salem Saeed Al Mohannadi, the founder of the first classic car museum in Qatar, has been collecting classic cars locally and from countries around the globe since the 1990s. His museum, located at his family farm, which one can get to after a serene drive up to the north of Qatar, has been open since 1999. In 2020, he expanded his collection to include works of art, archival material, and rare photographs.

SABAAN MESMAR AL JASSIM MUSEUM AND SHOP

Souq Waqif
Sabaan Mesmar Al Jassim has been collecting antiques of all types, mostly related to Qatar, but also the Arab region, for over 50 years. He has had a store in the historic Souq Waqif for decades, where he displays his collection of books, photographs, letters, medals, rare rocks, and so much more, as well as selling antiques. Visitors will also find craftsmen working on traditional memorabilia, such as miniature dhow boats. Outside, there is a spectacular array of larger objects, including giant desert roses, pearl diving equipment—and a fishing boat.

LETBELAH CAR MUSEUM

Al Khor and Al Thakhira Municipality
Letbelah is the local term for a "shaded garage", and is the name Omar Hussain Alfardan chose for his museum at his family's farm. Letbelah's collection includes rare cars from the makers for whom the Alfardan family is the dealer in Qatar, such as Ferrari, BMW, Rolls Royce and Jaguar. The oldest goes back to the early 1900s, and all have been maintained to ensure they can be driven. In fact, Omar, his brother Fahad, and friends have been seen driving the cars on weekends along the Northern Highway, stopping at heritage sites for the public to admire them.

ABDULLAH AL GHANIM MUSEUM

Fereej Al Ghanim
This charming museum in a private house has been established by Abdulla Shaheen Ghanem Al Ghanim Al Maadeed. It focuses on the heritage of Qatar and the Arabian Gulf, and displays more that 500 ethnographic objects, documents, photographs, and artworks. Many of the objects have been gifts from family members, who have nurtured and supported Al Maadeed's passion for heritage and collecting. The museum provides a unique inside view of traditional Qatari life. There are plans to extend the museum to examine the interiors and exteriors of Qatari houses.

MUSEUMS

Exhibitions calendar 2022–2024

As Qatar prepares for the FIFA World Cup 2022™, Qatar Museums is inaugurating an array of temporary exhibitions at museums and a multitude of other sites around the country, details of which are below. Many of the shows for fall 2022 are part of the Qatar-MENASA 2022 Year of Culture program (see p29). In the World Cup year, QM has greatly expanded this annual initiative of bilateral exchange to celebrate the cultures of two dozen nations of the MENASA region. Here is a list of our current exhibitions and upcoming shows in 2023 and 2024. As more programs are added by our Years of Culture partners, some dates are subject to change. Please refer to the #QatarCreates and Qatar Museums websites for current updates.

MUSEUMS

3-2-1 OLYMPIC AND SPORTS MUSEUM

World of Football
October 2, 2022–April 1, 2023
The *World of Football* exhibition celebrates the historic occasion of Qatar hosting the FIFA World Cup 2022™. The first half, *Football for All, All for Football*, examines the universal appeal of the beautiful game, as played, watched, and enjoyed by millions. The second half, *The Road to Doha*, follows the journey to Qatar 2022, from the first FIFA World Cup™ matches in Uruguay in 1930, to the final at the Lusail Stadium on December 18, 2022. A "FIFA Making Memories" section will emerge during the exhibition, as items are added to record events at the FIFA World Cup 2022™.

Also
Digital Sports Games *September–December 2023*

FIRE STATION

Experience Al Jazeera
October 19, 2022–March 25, 2023
Over the past 25 years, Al Jazeera Media Network has grown from a single TV channel to a global media phenomenon. The exhibition explores the meteoric trajectory of Al Jazeera, its emphasis on the human story, its editorial integrity, creative processes, and technology. Through interactive exhibits such as a "Studio Experience", visitors can see a studio setting first-hand. Special tours of Al Jazeera's headquarters can be booked through the Culture Pass and One Pass membership scheme.

Also
Alumni 6 Artist in Residency *May—August 2023*

M7

Forever Valentino
October 28, 2022–April 1, 2023
Maison Valentino pays homage to its founder with an exhibition curated by Massimiliano Gioni, artistic director of New Museum in New York and author and fashion critic Alexander Fury at M7 in the Msheireb neighborhood. *Forever Valentino* will be Maison Valentino's largest show to date and its first presentation in the Middle East.

Also
Vitra – 100 Masterpieces of Furniture Design
September–December 2023

L'École: Around the World in Jewelry
October 2023–March 2024

MATHAF

Inspired by the Land
Until January 21, 2023
Drawing on talented emerging Qatari artist Al Maha Al Maadeed's cultural memory and family history, *Inspired by the Land* questions the effects of urbanization in Qatar. Featured works demonstrate the process of contextualizing family archives using poetry and oral literature.

~~INVISIBLE LABORS~~ daydream therapy
September 16, 2022–January 21, 2023
Bringing together existing and new works for Qatari-American artist Sophia Al Maria's first large-scale, multi-part museum show in the Middle East, this project sees Al Maria inviting artists, curators, scholars, and communities to discuss histories, dreaming, futures, and the Gulf's relation to surrounding regions. Featuring a range of media including installation, video pieces, and commissioned soundscapes, the show foregrounds the importance of storytelling as a strategy of survival. The exhibition is part of the Qatar-MENASA 2022 Year of Culture.

No Condition is Permanent
Until January 21, 2023
This show surveys the work of Gaza-born artist Taysir Batniji created between 1997 and 2022. During this period, Batniji lived in France, but his life and work meditate on Palestine. While the exhibition title refers to a single artwork, pieces on display look at Batniji's diverse practice using drawing photography, video, installation, and performance. The exhibition is part of the Qatar-MENASA 2022 Year of Culture.

Majaz: Contemporary Art Qatar
Until February 25, 2023
This exhibition celebrates five years of the artist-in-residence (AIR) program at the Fire Station. In January 2021, the Fire Station invited 14 AIR alumni to participate in the six-month-long development of works for the show, which features an additional 25 former residents, showcasing

Untitled (1975) by Baya Mahieddine, one of the works that will be shown at the Qatar National Library this October as part of an exhibition devoted to the late artist.

MUSEUMS

Top: Taysir Batniji's installation, *Hannoun*, will appear at Mathaf's *No Condition is Permanent* until January 2023.
Above: Ahmed Mahood's *Iraqi Wedding* features in MIA's upcoming *Baghdad: Eye's Delight* exhibition.

works in a variety of discipline. The works are displayed in dialogue to highlight elements of storytelling. The exhibition is part of the Qatar-MENASA 2022 Year of Culture.

One Tiger or Another
Until January 21, 2023
This is a show about stories, histories, and the ways in which we invent and reinvent ourselves and others. The story begins with the 18th-century South Indian ruler Tipu Sultan, also known as the "Tiger of Mysore", a figure who has been variously celebrated as a hero of Indian resistance to foreign colonialism, and a cruel tyrant. These contrasting opinions are traced through exquisite objects commissioned or owned by Tipu, and ephemera from more contemporary cultures that perpetuate one or another reading of his mythology. This is a project by Rubaiyat Qatar.

Beirut and the Golden Sixties – A Manifesto of Fragility
March 19–August 5, 2023
Conceived as a central part of the Lyon Contemporary Art Biennale, the exhibition revisits a dazzling chapter from Beirut's modern history between 1958 and 1978. With more than 225 artworks and 300 archival documents from 36 collections in 16 cities worldwide, it highlights Beirut's pivotal role in elaborating a vision for modernity through a politically engaged art where everything seemed possible. The exhibition is curated by Sam Bardaouil and Till Fellrath, who were responsible for *Tea with Nefertiti* (2013) and Mona Hatoum's *Turbulence* (2014), both hosted at Mathaf, and the Lebanese Pavilion at the 55th Venice Biennale (2013).

MUSEUM OF ISLAMIC ART

October 2022
The opening of the reimagined Museum of Islamic Art, with new thematic galleries and a new family trail. The reopening coincides with the inauguration of the Civic Flag Plaza, in neighboring MIA Park.

Baghdad: Eye's Delight
October 26, 2022–February 25, 2023
An exhibition celebrating Baghdad as the most important and influential city ever created in the Islamic world. The display takes the visitor on an imaginary tour across centuries, highlighting Baghdad's role as a city of power, scholarship, and commerce—both under the Abbasids and, again, in the mid 20th century. The journey ends with a look at the city's social fabric, its cosmopolitan population and many traditions, which have—despite war and destruction—enabled the city to thrive, time and time again. The exhibition features objects on loan from 22 lenders including the Louvre, the Metropolitan Museum of Art, and the Vatican. The exhibition is part of the Qatar-MENASA 2022 Year of Culture.

Raku
From November 2022
Raku is a type of Japanese pottery made using the Raku firing process, in which the piece is hand-molded instead of being turned on a potter's wheel and fired at a low temperature. The works displayed in the main entrance corridor of MIA are made using sand and other minerals from the Qatari desert, and reference the people and culture of Qatar, as well as the poetry of the nation's founder, Sheikh Jassim.

Also
Mosque Exhibition *March–August 2023*

Fashioning an Empire: Safavid Textiles from the Museum of Islamic Art *October 2023–January 2024*

MIA PARK

Afghanistan
October 2022
This exhibition highlights Qatar's enduring commitment to Afghanistan, to the preservation of its rich culture and history, and the promise of a dignified and prosperous future for the country and its people. The relationship, past, present, and future, is set against a backdrop that pays tribute to and exposes the value of Afghanistan's diverse artistic, cultural, natural, and scientific heritage.

Yayoi Kusama: My Soul Blooms Forever
October 23, 2022–March 3, 2023
Well-known for her repeating dot patterns, the art of Japan's Yayoi Kusama encompasses an astonishing variety of media, including painting, drawing, sculpture, film, performance, and immersive installation. In this open-air show sculptures by Kusama will be scattered throughout the park, palm trees will be draped and dotted, and there will be an infinity room, and a gift shop.

NATIONAL MUSEUM OF QATAR

Pipilotti Rist: Your Brain to Me, My Brain to You
Until January 14, 2023
This is a large-scale immersive installation by internationally renowned Swiss artist Pipilotti Rist. Commissioned by the National Museum to meet the unique dimensions of its gallery, it invites visitors to embark on a journey of self-discovery through a multisensory experience that inspires introspection and awe. A key feature of the work is "pixels" that comprise 12,000 LEDs throughout the gallery for visitors to navigate. Representing neurons, constantly firing and communicating with each other, the pulsing bulbs have been programmed in a choreography with a soundscape and abstract footage of Qatari landscapes.

A Sneak Peek at Qatar Auto Museum Project
Until 2025
This small exhibition, with three cars and information panels, introduces the forthcoming Qatar Auto Museum. It explores the significance of automotive design in the 20th century and the impact of automobiles on culture.

MUSEUMS

157

Qatar Auto Museum has also installed 10 racing cars at 10 different heritage sites (until January 2023). The cars are displayed in repurposed shipping containers.

On the Move
October 27, 2022–January 7, 2023
On the Move explores the lives of nomadic and semi-nomadic pastoralists across three distinct geographical regions: Central Sahara, Qatar, and Mongolia. The exhibition examines how these groups maintain rich and meaningful social lives while producing complex and beautiful cultural forms in some of the most challenging environments. The show features a rich selection of objects, historical images, and archival footage from the collections of the National Museum of Qatar and other QM collections, along with loans from a number of international museums including the National Museum of Mongolia, Musée du Quai Branly, and Weltmuseum Vienna.

Also
Olafur Eliasson *March–August 2023*

The Shape of Time: Art and Ancestors of Oceania from the Metropolitan Museum of Art *October 2023–January 2024*

Mal Lawal *October 4, 2023–January 2024*

Countryside: The Future, Chapter II
November 2023–January 2024

QATAR FLOUR MILL WAREHOUSE AND AL NAJADA HERITAGE HOUSE #15

Art Mill Museum 2030
October 24, 2022–April 1, 2023
The Art Mill Museum is not due to open for another eight years but, in the meantime, this exhibition introduces what will eventually be Qatar's home of international modern and contemporary art. It presents an overview of the scheme designed by the studio ELEMENTAL, led by the Pritzker Prize-winning architect Alejandro Aravena. This part of the exhibition is at the industrial flour mill that will become the museum. A second part of the preview focuses on the creative village and gardens that are being designed by VOGT Landscape Architects, led by Günther Vogt; this can be seen at the recently restored Al Najada Heritage House #15, south of Wadi Msheireb Street.

QATAR NATIONAL LIBRARY

Baya Mahieddine
October 15, 2022–February 21, 2023
Highlighting works from the Qatar Museums collection, as well as from private collections and the National Library, this exhibition introduces the art of Baya Mahieddine, an Algerian artist who was discovered at age 16 after her first show at the Aimé Maeght gallery, Paris. Baya's paintings offer unique representations of flora and fauna.

QM GALLERY KATARA

Labor of Love: Embroidering Palestinian History
October 12, 2022–January 28, 2023
Labor of Love takes visitors on a journey of discovery of *tatreez* embroidery, as woven into the social, economic, and political fabric of Palestinian society. The exhibition examines the symbols of traditional embroidered Palestinian dress (*thobe*), and explores *tatreez* through the lenses of gender, labor, commodification, and class. The show traces the shift of *tatreez* from a personal practice to national symbol. The exhibition draws from the collections of Qatar Museums and the Palestinian Museum, and is part of the Qatar-MENASA 2022 Year of Culture.

Also
Wafika Sultan Al Essa & Hassan Al Mulla
September 2023–March 2024

QM GALLERY AL RIWAQ

Lusail Museum: Tales of a Connected World
October 24, 2022–April 1, 2023
Qatar Museums presents a special exhibition that introduces the museum designed by Herzog & de Meuron, currently under development in Lusail. This preview shows how the museum will draw on QM's world-class collection of art, archaeological artifacts, and media from prehistoric times to the 21st century to create a new, enlightened, and constructive way of understanding who we in the Arab world are, where we come from, and where we are going.

FESTIVALS

Design Doha
February–May 2024

A biannual festival for Qatar, Design Doha is a platform for local, regional, and global design excellence in the form of a concentrated week of events, plus further programming. The festival will be anchored by two headline exhibitions, provisionally titled *Future Designs* and *Arab Design Now*. The former will be co-curated by American artist and architect Daniel Arsham, the latter by Rana Beiruti, founding director of the Amman Design Festival, Jordan.

Doha Film Experience
November 22–December 16, 2022

As part of the Ajyal Film Festival 2022, DFI's eclectic line-up of screenings include family favorites, film classics, and thematic offerings. There will also be a special program linking the Museum of Islamic Art's *Baghdad: Eye's Delight* exhibition, as well as a selection of short and feature films that showcase the greatest voices emerging from MENASA independent cinema. See the DFI website for details. This exhibition is part of the Qatar-MENASA 2022 Year of Culture.

Top: A concept sketch from the Art Mill Museum 2030 exhibition taking place at the Qatar Flour Mill Warehouse, from October 2022.
Above: From October, NMoQ will examine nomadic and semi-nomadic groups across Central Sahara, Qatar, and Mongolia.

Mother's Embrace (2013) by Nabil Anani will be shown at the QM Gallery Katara from October as part of the *Labor of Love: Embroidering Palestinian History* exhibition.

Festival in Motion
December 5–18, 2022

Curated by choreographer Benjamin Millepied and composer Nico Muhly, this festival consists of 55 performances across 10 locations. It will feature world premieres and site-specific stagings from at least 15 artists, and more than 50 performers. Visit qacreates.com

Geekdom
December 3–16, 2022

Part of the Ajyal Film Festival, this is Qatar's largest one-of-a-kind pop culture program. It will run at the Lusail Boulevard, bringing together lovers of technology and anime. See the DFI website for details.

Intaj
November 8–December 16, 2022

A multimedia exhibition organized by the Doha Film Institute at Msheireb Galleria, it showcases the evolution of Qatari cinema, TV drama, and live theater through archival materials, historical objects, multidisciplinary artists, and the involvement of the community.

Rubaiyat
October 2024–March 2025

Rubaiyat is a multidisciplinary quadrennial exhibition launching its first edition in 2024. It aims to explore the nature of art in the broadest possible sense. Leading up to the event there will be a series of pop-up exhibitions, and a program of art and writing residencies. Storytelling, in oral and written form, will be at the heart of the first festival. It is intended that Rubaiyat 2024 will take the form of a multisite exhibition across Qatar, occupying conventional exhibition spaces, as well as heritage sites, sites of ecological and environmental interest, and shopping malls.

Tasweer Photo Festival
March–May 2023

This second edition of Qatar Museums photo festival features a dynamic program of awards, commissions, public debates, workshops, and indoor and outdoor displays. A highlight is the exhibition of the winners in the Sheikh Saud Al Thani Awards, which supports work from photographers resident in Western Asia and North Africa. Sites used include Al Koot Fort, Al Najada House and Al Rayyan Palace.

FASHION

CR Qatar Fashion United
December 16, 2022

CR Qatar Fashion United is a monumental celebration of fashion, culture, and music. Conceived by al-Mayassa bint Hamad bin Khalifa Al-Thani and curated by Carine Roitfeld, the epic fashion show will feature over 100 brands, from the world's most acclaimed fashion designers to emerging designers from five continents. With representations from more than 50 countries and the world's biggest names in modeling, the global event will also include a concert featuring performances by top international musical artists. It will benefit the Education Above All Foundation, a non-profit organization that gives vulnerable children access to education.

THEATER

Monsoon Wedding
November 15–28, 2022

This is the musical of the 2001 film of the same name, an Indian comedy-drama depicting romantic entanglements during a traditional Punjabi Hindu wedding in Delhi. The film's director, Mira Nair, also directs this production. Performances take place at the Abdul Aziz Nasser Theater in Souq Waqif.

MUSEUMS

4

THE QATAR

4

BLUE PRINT

our national assets: heritage sites, farms, and youth

PLANNING THE FUTURE

Before the pandemic, I was living with my husband and children in New York. When Covid hit, my father asked us to return to Doha. Qatar was a leader in managing the outbreak because the government implemented strict and effective control policies. And because Qatar's weather is favorable for most of the year, families could spend their time in quarantine outdoors.

It was during this period that I joined the Doha Environmental Actions Project (DEAP), an organization run by Jose Saucedo, a Mexican national living in Qatar who motivates students and community members to go out and clean the beaches. My children and I enjoyed participating in this. At one point, we were going every Thursday to clean up a heritage site; my children were on a hybrid school program so I would take whoever was home that day. The drives through the deserts and the hours spent cleaning up the villages and beaches were not only important for our environment but gave us some quality family time. In having our children witness and participate first-hand in the responsibilities they have toward the planet, we are giving them the necessary tools to be environmental soldiers.

I realized that as an adult, unlike in my childhood, I had spent most of my summers abroad, and between work and raising my five children, I almost forgot about the wealth of Qatar's heritage, natural sites, and rare animal species. My experiences with the #keepqatarclean campaign led me to invite municipal leaders, organizations such as Salem Al Mohannadi's Seashore Group—one of our biggest supporters—and members of environmental youth clubs to join us in these clean-ups. Not only was it important to look after our beaches and other areas, but it was also crucial for us to discuss how we could prevent more damage and keep pollution out of our lands and seas.

Qatar is home to hawksbill turtles, the Arabian oryx, dugongs, flamingos, whale sharks, the rarest birds, and much more. A lot of the mammals here are endangered, so it is essential to keep their habitats clean and understand how to co-exist with them. For example, dugongs are shy and people should not go near or disturb them, whereas whale sharks welcome humans swimming alongside them. In fact, Qatar Tourism recently introduced whale shark visits at the Al Shaheen Oil Field that typically run from May to August.

Another program born out of the pandemic is the turtle-hatching encounter initiative, where participants observe experts as they release newly hatched turtles into the sea. The scheme focuses on the hawksbill sea turtles, a critically endangered species that maintains the health of coral reefs and the marine ecosystem. At a sanctuary at Fuwairit Beach in the north of Qatar, they nest and lay from 60 to 200 eggs between April and August. The area is usually closed to the public, but because of our relationships with the Ministry of Environment, Qatar University, and Qatar Energy, Qatar Museums Culture Pass Members can access it to learn about these reptiles and how to protect them. Within two hours of announcing the initiative to our members, all the offered spots were taken. I took my children to witness the process, and very much encourage families to do the same. We have now opened the turtle-hatching program to the public so they know what to do should they find baby turtles wondering outside the protected reserve.

Another unique experience that combines both nature and heritage is a visit to Al Maha Sanctuary, which breeds the Arabian oryx—a small antelope that was almost extinct until my husband's grandfather, Sheikh Jassim bin Hamad Al Thani, who was an uncle of my father, started to collect, breed and protect them.

THE QATAR BLUEPRINT

The turtle-hatching initiative at Fuwairit Beach shows people what to do if they find baby hawksbill sea turtles outside of the protected reserve area

I am hoping that his great-grandchildren will take on the same responsibility to nurture the environment.

Our current National Vision 2030 aims to transform Qatar into an advanced country by the end of this decade, capable of sustaining its own development and providing a high standard of living for its population and future generations. Its pillars are human, social, economic, and environmental development. We are now looking beyond that date with our Qatar Blueprint. This is a new national initiative to plan our future from within, dividing the municipalities into seven distinct zones and identifying all our heritage and nature assets in each of them. Through different conversations with researchers and environmentalists, I have learned that we have a lot of work to do. But being effective means involving all parties. We need to engage both government and non-government sectors, Qataris and residents, to protect and enhance the natural habitats we have inherited. Moving beyond the World Cup in 2022, we will engage all relevant parties in discussions and workshops to align our efforts toward building Qatar's vision beyond 2030.

With so much to offer, and so many stories to revisit, the prospect of planning the future with culture, heritage, and nature at the core excites and motivates me. In the following pages, I cannot cover all our natural and heritage sites, but I have selected a few of these as well as some farms that I have visited during my many #keepqatarclean efforts. It is my wish for you to enjoy what my country has to offer, and participate in keeping it clean. For more sites, farms and future activations please continue to visit us on our #QatarCreates website.

PALACES AND
HERITAGE HOUSES

Qatar is a country with a rich heritage, there for all to see in its numerous palaces, historical houses, archaeological sites, and heritage villages. Qatar's location on a peninsula placed it on significant trade routes, which brought people of different backgrounds together, creating epicenters of knowledge. Some of these sites are well known—Al Zubarah, for instance—but many are not. Working closely with former owners and inhabitants, Qatar Museums is giving many heritage sites—houses and villages—new practical uses. We are collaborating with families connected to the sites not only to restore buildings, but to preserve and present their family histories, going back as long as possible. These local contributions are critical for future generations to understand how their ancestors lived.

Many of these sites are in the north of the country, which is a region I highly recommend everybody to visit. This can be done as a day trip, or you can stay overnight. As well as heritage sites, there is art and numerous options for play. Our new Kite Surfing Club, for example, located in the windiest part of the country, attracts kite surfers from around the globe. Other water activities, including kayaking, sailing and paddle boarding, can be organized by a number of service providers. Back on dry land, I personally recommend renting bikes (I like my electric off-road bike and spend hours on it exploring my country). For those looking for a more relaxing time, the newly opened wellness center of Zulal, managed by Chiva-Som, is the ultimate destination.

On the following pages I would like to introduce you to some of the places that, if time allows, visitors to Qatar should consider seeing and experiencing. Over the next few years, a greater emphasis will be put on excavating more of our heritage sites and linking them into our Qatar Blueprint.

Al Rayyan Palace

This residence—or rather, grouping of residences within a walled compound—belonged to my grandfather, his father, and his brothers. My maternal grandmother lived here when she was first married and, later, my father would spend some of his childhood years here. Today, the original architecture of the compound has been preserved. As part of the Tasweer 2021 Photography Festival, the curator Maryam Hassan Al-Thani displayed photographs by the Qatari photographer Shaha Al Khulaifi inside one of the buildings. I took my youngest son to visit the installation, and it was beautiful to see site-specific contemporary photography engage with the old palace. The site will be re-used for Tasweer 2023.

Ali bin Abdullah Palace

The Ali bin Abdullah Palace belonged to a former Amir of Qatar. I have heard many stories of relatives visiting the residence to see Sheikh Ali bin Abdullah. I hosted one of the Reach Out to Asia galas here, and all the participants were inspired by the beautifully renovated space. During the FIFA World Cup 2022™, the palace will be used as one of the transit hubs for VIP guests. After the tournament, we hope to make this venue available for special events.

Fahad bin Ali Palace

The historic palace, once belonging to the son of an Amir of Qatar, is located behind the Amiri Diwan and opposite the new Qasr Al Hukum museum. It was recently converted into Qatar Museums' archaeological headquarters. Appropriately, it has a preserved Ottoman graveyard.

Bayt Al Khulaifi

The Bayt Al Khulaifi compound was built in 1940 by Mubarak Al Khulaifi, and was one of the few houses constructed next to the palace of Sheikh Abdullah bin Jassim—which is the historical residence that is now part of the National Museum of Qatar. The original Al Khulaifi family have taken over the building and turned it into Bayt Sharq, a traditional restaurant that serves breakfast, lunch, and dinner.

Al Najada and Al Asmakh Houses

These are two of Qatar Museums' latest restoration projects, taking place in neighboring heritage districts just south of Msheireb and Souq Waqif in Downtown Doha. On the occasion of the FIFA World Cup 2022™, one of the restored houses in Al Najada will showcase the gardens of the future Art Mill Museum project, while houses in Al Asmakh will support the designer and entrepreneur residency initiatives started by the M7 and Liwan design centers. In the future, we hope to make these houses available for small and medium businesses interested in contributing to the creative economy.

Al Zaman House Numismatic Center

Located in Doha's Old Ghanim neighborhood, Al Zaman House is a beautifully renovated 1950s heritage building that will become a leading center of Islamic coins, as Qatar Museums owns one of the largest coin collections. The house will feature an exhibition space to explore the history of life in Al Zaman house and the surrounding area, as well as being a center where visitors can learn about Islamic currencies and contemporary monetary management.

Traditional restaurant Bayt Sharq now occupies the former site of the Bayt Al Khulaifi compound.

An aerial view of Al Zubarah archaeological site, Qatar's first World Heritage location.

Al Zubarah and Ain Mohammed

Al Zubarah is a UNESCO World Heritage Site in northern Qatar and one of the most significant heritage sites in Qatar. A once-thriving 18th-century pearl trading port, at its peak it boasted an impressive city wall, residential palaces and houses, markets, mosques, and a fort. Little of that survives, but the archaeological remains provide an invaluable insight into early urban planning and traditional Qatari building techniques. Digs here have also uncovered evidence of the harmonious coexistence of different cultures and ethnic groups. There is a well-restored fort at the site, which dates from 1938 and the reign of Sheikh Abdullah bin Jassim Al Thani. The fort was used as a coastguard station until the 1980s before being transformed into a museum.

Not far from Al Zubarah are art installations by Olafur Eliasson, Simone Fattal, and Ernesto Neto, all linked by a trail that encourages visitors to explore the area by hiking and biking. The trail finishes at Ain Mohammed, a village recently restored by descendants of its original inhabitants, the Nuaim tribe. Ain Mohammed has tents available for overnight stays, providing an authentic immersion in Bedouin culture. For those looking for adventure, horse and camel excursions can be organized. There are also other historic forts and sites within the region, including Al Rakayat and Al Thagab forts and the Abbasid-era settlements of Murwab and Ruwanda.

Al Ruwais Police Station

Built in 1955, the police station is located at the northern tip of Al Ruwais village. Historically, police stations such as this were built near harbors for security reasons. They also served as custom

THE QATAR BLUEPRINT

posts, monitoring boat traffic as it left town. Today, it is the Arsan Café, operated by Sheikha Al Sada since 2019, and is always busy, especially on Fridays.

Al Jassasiya

Fascinating rock carvings or petroglyphs can be found at around a dozen sites along Qatar's coast, but the largest concentration (more than 900) are on a low limestone ridge at Al Jassasiya, north of Doha. Discovered in 1957, experts believe they are thousands of years old. The most common motifs are round holes, but what they represent is unknown. Some are carved in a seemingly random order, while others are cut in rows and feature motifs such as rosettes and stars. There are also carvings of boats, fish, scorpions, ostriches and footprints. As well as private homes, the area boasts the famous Al Maroona beach, where people can kite surf and camp.

Al Khor

North-east of Doha is the city of Al Khor, which is the home of my mother's Al Misned family. It has one of the main venues for the FIFA World Cup 2022™, Al Bayt Stadium. The Olympic cycling track—at 33km, the world's longest—links Doha to the stadium and is a popular route for bikers. One of its 29 underpasses has recently been transformed with a mural celebrating the contributions of those who have helped to build the infrastructure of hotels, stadiums, roads, hospitals, and much more.

Al Khor, with its impressive corniche and historic souq, is also the gateway to the Bin Ghannam Island mangroves, which can be explored by kayak. Flamingos can be seen during the winter season. Recent excavations in the region have unearthed millions of crushed shells belonging to the sea snail *Thais savignyi*, along with large ceramic vats that were probably used to macerate the mollusks. This type of shellfish produces a dark red-purple dye—the color of our flag.

Al Wakrah

Al Wakrah is south of Doha, and not too far from Hamad International Airport. It is the second largest urban area in Qatar after Doha. Historically an important trading center, the town has an enormous, maze-like souq and one of the country's best beaches. It is also home to Zaha Hadid's Al Janoub Stadium, the form of which was inspired by the dhow, the boat that was once central to life in the region. Zaha was a friend and an inspiration to me, as the only Arab Muslim woman to lead an international architectural practice. She worked with us on a tents exhibition that is currently on view at the National Museum.

Khor Al Udaid

Khor Al Udaid is a beautiful "inland sea"—although it is actually a creek—in the far south-east of the country on the border with Saudi Arabia. It is a UNESCO-recognized nature reserve with diverse scenery of exceptional, undeveloped natural beauty. The fauna includes several species that are internationally rare and/or threatened, such as the dugong. There are also Arabian gazelles, and lots of visiting migrant waterfowl and regionally declining breeding species, including ospreys. If you are looking for an intimate resort, I would recommend a meal at the Al Majles Resort developed by Khalid Al Suwaidi, an entrepreneur who also runs Doha Bus Adventures.

THE QATAR BLUEPRINT

FARM LIFE

I spent most weekends of my childhood and young adult life at the family farm. Farms are an important part of Qatar's community culture, with many families having their own private farms inherited from their ancestors. Recently, many of these have been opened to the public so they can appreciate the importance of agriculture. To spend the weekend at a farm helps one reconnect to nature. Today, many of our children are unaware of where the food they eat comes from. But by going to the farms and participating in planting, milking goats, collecting eggs, and seeing the sheep and goats, they might gain some awareness of the food cycle, and make more conscious decisions on what they eat. As you explore the country outside Doha, all the following farms welcome visitors.

Torba Farm

Torba is a family farm in the north of Qatar run by Mohammed Al Khater, who is the proprietor of the Sidra House pharmacy across from the Sidra Hospital. In my many conversations with Mohammed, I have been inspired by his knowledge of local plants, which he uses to produce essential oils, teas, and natural remedies. There is a market and a store, the latter offering a range of products, including eco-friendly cleaners, healthcare items, and fresh local vegetables, plus an eatery specializing in nutritious seasonal dishes. Back in Doha, since 2017, Fatma Al Khater has run the Torba Farmer's Market every weekend in Education City. This is the first artisanal and plastic-free farmer's market in the country.

Baladna Farm

Operated by the Al Khayat family, Baladna Farm is near Al Bayt Stadium, in Al Khor, which is hosting several of the FIFA World Cup 2022™ games. The farm started during the blockade, in response to Saudi Arabia stopping food from coming across our shared land border. The farm owns over 24,000 cows, with the Baladna brand featuring some of Qatar's best dairy products, and also operates shops and restaurants in Doha. It featured in Rem Koolhaas's *Countryside* exhibition, which ran at the Guggenheim Museum in New York in 2020, and is coming to Doha in October 2023.

Heenat Salma Farm

Heenat Salma Farm is just outside Doha, near Al Shahaniya camel racetrack. It recently opened to the public after Fahad Al Attiya (who is currently Qatar's ambassador to the UK) took it over. He knows the importance of quality produce and healthy eating, having previously led Qatar's food security initiative, bringing the COP 18 climate conference to Qatar. The farm grows around 30 different crops of fruit and vegetables, all organic, in addition to producing eggs, honey, and meat and dairy products. Heenat Salma also runs wellness and creative programs, and has recently partnered with the Katara Art Center in Doha. The farm offers creative residencies, and has lodges for people who wish to stay overnight.

Mohammed Abdulmehsin Al Fayad Farm

Mohammed Abdulmehsin Al Fayad's Farm is a hidden gem in the northern desert of Qatar near historic Al Thagab Fort (recently restored by Qatar Museums). Notable for its distinctive buildings, constructed from local *froosh* stone, the majority of the farm is solar powered, which Mohammed installed himself. He also used recycled elements in the farm's buildings. Visitors can be accommodated overnight, when they will often be entertained by Mohammed, and possibly get to meet some of his grandchildren.

North Sedra Farm

Reached by an off-road drive to the west of Al Shamal highway, cruising through desert landscapes, visitors arrive at the North Sedra Farm already feeling a sense of release from urban life. It is run by Mohammed Ajlan Al Kaabi, his wife Maryam Abdulla Al Kaabi, and their children, who have all helped in transforming an old family farm into a destination open to the public during winter season weekends. A family-run museum in the grounds, curated mostly by Maryam, includes objects related to everyday Qatari life, past and present, and features a section on the "firsts of Qatar"— the first female minister, the first Qatari music band, the first TV presenter. The farm has peacocks, gazelles, camels, llamas, ducks, pigeons, turtles, sheep, zebras, and more, plus a petting zoo for kids. There is fruit and vegetable picking, including a native fruit known as *knar* (it's like a tiny apple). All activities are accompanied by tour guides who share with families their wealth of knowledge about the farm.

Al Dosari Farm and Zoo

In the central region of Qatar known as Al Shahaniya, the Dosari family has transformed an old farm in the desert into a nature reserve for all kinds of animals, both native and from the wider region. The farm has a breeding program aimed at increasing Qatar's wild population of certain animals. Guest activities include horse and camel riding, and fresh-water fish feeding. There are also museum-like sections covering media and heritage. The reserve includes cabins for overnight stays.

Al Wabra Farm

Al Wabra Farm, an oasis of green areas and palm trees, belonged to the late Sheikh Saud bin Mohammed Al Thani. During his life,

I visited him here many times. The property has the only Philip Johnson building in the region, as well as the rarest breeds of endangered wildlife, cared for by an international team of expert vets, biologists, and keepers brought in by Sheikh Saud. Traditional antelopes and gazelles can be found in great numbers here, as can birds of paradise. Some of the Sheikh's love of nature was recently captured in an exhibition at the Museum of Islamic Art called *The Eye of a Falcon*, including beautiful photos of him with his gazelles taken by Richard Avedon. Sheikh Saud played a very important role in the foundation of the National Arts Council, and his passion for collecting heritage objects remains one of his lasting legacies. As this is a preservation site, public visits are limited, so it is worth booking a private visit via the farm's website.

As well as being a working farm that grows organic crops, Heenat Salma also offers accommodation in traditional tents.

INVESTING IN YOUTH

The 25-year strategy we initiated in 2005 with the establishment of Qatar Museums had as one of its primary goals the creation of a portfolio of world-class museums. But it wasn't only about buildings and physical infrastructure. It was also about people—specifically young people. As part of our planning, we are investing in young people to provide them with the knowledge needed to be part of this narrative, whether directly or indirectly. #QatarCreates has established a team of teenage volunteers, some of whom you will likely meet during the FIFA World Cup 2022™. We have also launched our Teenage Council, which is a permanent body of young people who will contribute to our future creative discourse and content creation. When my father abdicated in 2013, handing power to my brother, he would quote Ali bin Abi Talib: "Teach your children the best of what you have been taught for they have been created for a time different than yours." Each generation has its own needs and their voices must be heard and considered as we plan our future cultural institutions.

Our museums have always put young people at the heart of what they do. The reopening of the Museum of Islamic Art will include a permanent space for teenagers on the fourth floor, and a new family trail intended to fully engage children in learning about the history of Islamic civilization. The National Museum has specific children's areas where kids can play and learn about the topics covered in the galleries. The 3-2-1 Olympic and Sports Museum has the highly interactive Activation Zone, which is all about fun, while Mathaf has multiple arts and literacy workshops and an annual student exhibition to showcase the talent we have in the country. Then, of course, we have the forthcoming Dadu Museum, which is wholly dedicated to children of all ages. This includes the Dadu Garden, which opens in the fall of 2022, and will be community-built and run, with local families invited to participate in its planting. It will include an edible kitchen, encouraging parents and children to establish healthy lifestyles. Embracing our ethos of connectivity, we chose to place the garden in a public park (Al Bidda) not far from the Fire Station's artists-in-residency center, to link creatives with what we are doing at Dadu.

That link will be given physical form when Qatar hosts the International Horticultural Expo in October 2023 in a building that has been developed for the occasion and which sits in the space between the new Dadu building and the Fire Station. After the Expo, this building will be incorporated into the Dadu program and have two roles: during the day it will operate as a school that focuses on museums and creativity; after hours it will become a place for teenagers and teachers to learn how to utilize museums for their various subjects. For now, the Dadu Garden will introduce the work of the Expo with an ambitious agenda explaining how local communities and regional and international audiences can improve our world. To support this objective, we are organizing two exhibitions: one with Rem Koolhaas on the countryside at the Qatar Preparatory School site in October 2023, and the second by Olafur Eliasson, which focuses on what our nation needs to do to help the environment, and which will open at the National Museum of Qatar in March 2023.

Like everywhere in the world, pollution continues to have an impact on the environment, especially the sea, and Qatar is a peninsula. The recent UN Climate Report reflects the urgency of the situation, and we all have a responsibility to act. Through our museum platforms and programs, Qatar Museums will continue to engage and raise awareness of these issues. Qatar's youth are leading the way with their own initiatives to reduce waste and pollution in our beautiful heritage villages and on the beaches. As a resident or visitor to Qatar, and a citizen of the world, please be aware that you have a contribution to make in improving the state of the planet for future generations and protecting the animals that are becoming extinct on a daily basis.

In the run-up to the FIFA World Cup 2022™, the Supreme Committee for Delivery & Legacy has worked to ensure Qatar is ready to welcome the world for the tournament, coordinating everything from the building of stadiums and infrastructure to the establishment of sustainability goals. We have created an ecological committee, open to all stakeholders in both private and public spheres and grassroots organizations, to discuss and improve the ways we are doing things. This committee will continue to work on the issues at stake, supporting the International Horticultural Expo and other events in raising awareness of what needs to be accomplished.

During the World Cup we encourage everyone to refill water bottles to reduce waste—perhaps using one of Qatar Museums' special collectible bottles (see p57). During the FIFA Arab Cup, held in Qatar in December 2021, we ran a pilot scheme at one stadium where the workforce was given a water bottle. Data collected from this showed that shifting to a refillable water bottle can significantly reduce the total plastic waste collected. Consequently, our Public Works Authority, Ashghal, is currently installing 1,000 water fountains across Qatar.

In addition, with the support of architect Norman Foster and the Supreme Committee for Delivery & Legacy, we are dreaming about the possibility of transforming Lusail Stadium after the tournament into a food security program to meet the local need but also to support the World Food Program. Can you imagine what we can do together if we join forces, energies and knowledge in turning what could be potential white elephants into useful productive spaces?

Colorful shipping containers and a modular steel structure make up Stadium 974, designed by Spain's Fenwick Iribarren Architects. The 40,000-seat World Cup venue at Ras Abu Aboud is the first stadium designed to be fully demountable in FIFA World Cup™ history. It will be dismantled and reassembled in a new location after the tournament. The number 974 is the amount of containers used.

POWER

OF

CULT

THE FUTURE PODCAST

GLOBALIZING THE LOCAL, LOCALIZING THE GLOBAL

While writing these reflections, I felt it was important to engage with the people who are supporting the growth of our creative economy. These people are either living in Qatar, involved in our projects, or speaking about the importance of the work being done. Over the next few years, I will be conducting casual conversations with those who have had an impact in the relationship between global and local concepts we are trying to nurture in our country. The podcast series will include individuals from the worlds of art, architecture, design, fashion, and music, as well as Qatar Museums directors, curators, sports people, musicians, and members of my family—who are all helping to shape the future of this nation. I also plan to speak to those who have written about the influence of museums and cultural spaces when it comes to mental health and economic growth. I hope to make this a useful reference and resource for those planning their own creative economy centers. Our discussions will also cover the importance of investing in art— its power to connect people and bridge gaps of misunderstanding.

In many cases, these conversations reflect on how these individuals came to be involved with Qatar, revisiting the projects they undertook and talking about how they found their experiences. But they will also be forward-looking. This was certainly the case with one of my first discussions, with architect Rem Koolhaas. As well as designing two spectacular buildings in Qatar, Rem is taking the lead in the design of the Qatar Auto Museum and is helping to develop the Qatar Blueprint project, which will propel us beyond the Qatar National Vision 2030. Building on what we have already achieved—including all the projects described in this book—the Blueprint imagines the demands of the future and responds with urban planning and policy developments that ensure the continued growth and wellbeing of Qatar and those who live here.

Another of my early interviewees was renowned artist Olafur Eliasson. We met ahead of the unveiling of his major new commission in the north of Qatar, which takes place this fall. Olafur is an artist who believes in the vision of Qatar, and is working toward installing an exhibition at NMoQ next spring. Sophia Al Maria is a Qatari-American artist, filmmaker, and writer, who was named in *ArtReview* magazine's 2021 Power 100—an annual ranking of the most influential people in art. I have had the pleasure of knowing Sophia for many years and our conversation takes in her major exhibition at Mathaf this fall. Massimiliano Gioni is an Italian curator who this year brings *Forever Valentino* to M7. He previously curated the exhibitions of Takashi Murakami and Jeff Koons in Doha.

There are so many people to thank for the work that we have been able to do. The men and women who will be joining me in conversation resemble the mosaic of faces, the constellation that made Qatar the country it is today. I want to thank everyone in the organizations I am involved in for working day and night, and dedicating their time and energy to realize our vision. Some of these conversations have been transcribed in this book, the rest are found on my podcast on the #QatarCreates website.

THE POWER OF CULTURE PODCAST

CONVERSATIONS × OLAFUR ELIASSON

Olafur Eliasson is an Icelandic-Danish artist known for large-scale installation art employing elemental materials such as light, water, and air temperature to enhance the viewer's experience. He was the creator of *The Weather Project* at Tate Modern, London, in 2003, which has been described as "a milestone in contemporary art", and *The New York City Waterfalls* in 2008. His latest piece of site-specific art will be inaugurated in Qatar in October 2022, followed by an exhibition in March 2023 at NMoQ.

PODCAST CONVERSATIONS TRANSCRIBED

al-Mayassa bint Hamad bin Khalifa Al-Thani (MH)

with

Olafur Eliasson (OE)

MH We have a lot of conversations about the importance of culture and the power of art—why do you think culture is such an important sector?

OE I think that one of the unique things about the cultural sector is that it can host disagreement, it welcomes disagreement. In business or other sectors, if I may generalize a bit, it's normally considered a success if you sort of "nail it" and end up having the same opinion. But in most cultural spaces, if you do not agree, if I like this red color on that painting and you like the blue, we can still recognize each other's aesthetic choices and be friends. Museums and other spaces of culture have that capacity to host people's differences, not only their sameness. That is why I'm very interested in culture as a hospitable platform or framework in which we can meet across diverse backgrounds and worldviews and share our differences. Those differences may even allow us to better understand and connect with each other.

MH Would you say then that culture is the most democratic form of conversation, irrespective of political systems in place?

OE I do believe that museums hold the potential to become parliament-like, reaching out to everyone, make everyone feel seen, recognizing their perspectives. Culture is not for the few but is, or ideally should be, accessible to many. Coming into a museum – or another space of art, theatre, or literature – can allow all people to feel reflected or represented, to feel that their voice is being heard. And you will, hopefully, leave the museum feeling that something in the museum spoke to you, addressed concerns that are relevant to you. This is an ideal, of course. But my main point is to see cultural spaces as spaces of listening. It's a little bit like when we, a while back, discussed the new [Art Mill] museum you're doing with [Alejandro] Aravena. I think that one of the greatest potentials of building a new museum is to be able to consider who is currently not being heard. We need to give these voices a space in which to become heard.

MH You sit on our steering committee for the Art Mill Museum, which will contain modern and contemporary art, with Arab art at the heart of it. Why do you think contemporary and modern art is important in our part of the world?

OE There is a need for spaces in society where you can go and feel that your uncertainties are embraced, where you can go to just be with your thoughts and emotions and doubts you might have. Looking at a work of art is actually looking at your own way of looking at a work of art—and at the world. You can see your own way of seeing and this is, I think, a mode of listening to oneself. It's not easy—it's hard work! Going to the museum is not going to an amusement park. If you want to go to Disneyland, you should go to Disneyland. The art museum is about looking inwards, being with your inner landscape. It's not about escapism and sensationalism.

MH I remember when I first saw your work, and this was at the Brooklyn Bridge in New York, which is why I really wanted you to come to Qatar and do an installation like your waterfalls in New York, which never materialized. But why and how did you end up doing that installation at the Brooklyn Bridge?

OE *The New Your City Waterfalls* [2008] were commissioned by Public Art Fund—a private non-profit initiative, philanthropically organized around donations, which does artworks around the city. I made a proposal for a work in Manhattan, on the periphery, I wanted to work with water or light. At some point, I settled on working with waterfalls. When you're in Manhattan, the water—at least back then—seemed more of a negative space, like the void between Downtown and Brooklyn, for instance. There's just that flat void with water that you can sail on, but, other than that, it's not really detectable as a space. So I wanted to turn that negative space into something positive, a space that is recognized in itself. It was an attempt to claim back a space that has been taken for granted, and give it back to people.

MH I now understand better how you work, because initially I thought "if he did waterfalls in New York, why not do waterfalls in Qatar?" But it's very clear that you like to work with the natural ecosystem and try to enhance it. So, I invited you to Doha and it took you years to make it. I know you're one of the most in-demand artists. But once you came, things moved quickly and you got really invested and engaged with what we're doing. What did you think in the end?

OE Thank you for inviting me in the first place. As you'll remember, I started out by simply touring the museum, speaking with archaeologists, mineralogists, and geologists. I met scientists who worked with the desert, with its plants, birds, and so on. And we looked at heritage sites and historical sites. The more time I got to spend in Qatar, the better I understood the trajectory of the many, many stories that are piled up on top of each other. I was hosted by gaining access to a lot of information that I did not have before. I also, as you know, had various opportunities to raise issues that I disagreed with you about. I'm very grateful for the honest exchanges we've had on the climate emergency, for instance, but on many other topics, too.

MH We have these discussions all the time. Because Qatar, as you know, uses the wealth that it gets from gas to transform into a knowledge-based economy, and to invest heavily in reforms, education, culture, empowerment, and empowering individuals. And the creative economy is high on our agenda, as is the environment. Can you say something about the new sculpture that you've created in the desert in Qatar?

OE In visiting Qatar I essentially came closer and closer to the ground. I arrived from high up in a plane, then I landed, and then I traveled into the desert. I asked those around me to help me see what I'm actually standing on: what is this place? In the desert, such as in areas in Iceland, there is not much to direct your sense of scale, there are no trees, for instance. And gradually I realized that I'm not standing in what could be seen as being on the periphery of what is habitable, on empty, barren land. No, I'm standing in a rich landscape full of information, and history shows that there has been human activity here across millennia. All of these things brought me to visit a few sites around the country, but primarily I wanted to be close to sites of historical significance. That's how I came to choose the site.

MH We are actually inaugurating a heritage village, Ain Mohammed, where you have your new installation. We will have a family that will be managing this and teaching young adults the traditions of our ancestors, whether it's in camel riding, or falconry, or poetry. And then we have your very contemporary culture across from that.

OE The artwork that I've done is very abstract in a way and, you know, you might park your car and, from a distance, wonder, "What is this? Is this even really art?" But at some point you may realize that the most important element is the experience of the actual site. The artwork consists of a cluster of more than 20 giant mirrors elevated above ground and several meters across, almost like a canopy or a ceiling under which you can stand. You look up into the mirrors and all you see is the ground on which you're standing—and yourself looking up, of course. That, I think, gives you a very beautiful view of the sand and the stones and small plants and the life in the desert. Maybe the sand will be blowing around a tiny bit. I think if you're there by yourself or with a few friends, it's really quiet. It's beautifully hot, but you're in the shadow, and suddenly you see bird life and plants and the horizon is shimmering and it may feel like you're actually inside a Fata Morgana, a mirage. This is very much in the spirit of my work; I've been using light, humidity, temperature, natural environments, or natural phenomena. And you being there is, of course, the most important part.

Should you decide to stay for longer, despite the heat—which I welcome!—you will experience the movement of shadows across the ground as well as the movement of their reflections in the mirrors. What might have seemed to be a fixed village of mirrored spaces becomes a slow journey of shadows.

In my work generally, I look at the interconnectivity and entanglements that define the artwork in a specific site, in a specific time, and with the people who engage with it. And that goes for our lives, too. I'm fascinated by how we come into being through networks and assemblages—some visible to us, others invisible. We're inevitably dependent on others, both human and more-than-human, say the desert or the wind. Even our bodies are inhabited by myriad non-human entities, not least gut bacteria that has a strong positive impact on our wellbeing. The Indian author Amitav Ghosh puts this well in *The Nutmeg's Curse: Parables for a Planet in Crisis*: "It is known also that microorganisms influence moods, emotions, and the human ability to reason. So if it is true that the human ability to speak, and think, can only be actualized in the presence of other species, can it really be said that these faculties belong exclusively to humans?"

MH Where are you at with the name?

OE The title allows me to steer people's attention. To me, what is really important is the experience of the local environmental conditions, the sun, the wind, the heat, the light breeze, the way the sun travels across the sky. And I was very curious about the historical tradition of navigation in the desert, the stars at night, and the way that the sundial was important. So, the title is *Shadows travelling on the sea of the day*. It suggests that the artwork is not as such the steel structures, the mirrors, all the stuff in the desert. No, maybe the artwork is the consequences of this coming together of sun, sand, wind, steel, mirror, desert sounds, and visitors. Maybe the artwork is your experience of it.

MH I just learned recently about your early life as a breakdancer. Is that how you began your artistic career?

OE As a teenager, I already had an interest in becoming an artist, but I felt my hand danced with my pencil on the paper, and it wasn't really doing it for me, so I started breakdancing. It was a subculture that sort of popped up in Denmark at the time. Within a couple of years I got really good at it. What I learned was that I could change the space in which I was moving through dancing. It made me practice hard to achieve something, and that turned out to be a good learning process when I wanted to be an artist later.

MH So can we expect you to breakdance at the opening of your new sculpture?

OE Yeah. No. Maybe. Maybe the night after, or the night before. And maybe not breakdance. Maybe more like dance and break a leg.

CONVERSATIONS × REM KOOLHAAS

Rem Koolhaas is a Dutch architect who works like a conceptual artist, drawing on a seemingly endless reservoir of ideas. He is a co-founder of the Office for Metropolitan Architecture (OMA), and among his most notable works are the CCTV Headquarters in Beijing (2012) and Garage Museum of Contemporary Art in Moscow (2014). Koolhaas is also an urban thinker who has designed masterplans for, among other places, suburban Paris, the Libyan desert, and Hong Kong. In Qatar, OMA is responsible for the National Library and the headquarters of the Qatar Foundation. He is also building the future Qatar Auto Museum and working on the Qatar Blueprint.

PODCAST CONVERSATIONS TRANSCRIBED

al-Mayassa bint Hamad bin Khalifa Al-Thani (MH)

with

Rem Koolhaas (RK)

MH Thank you so much for your time. I have always been fascinated by the trajectory of your life, the many experiences and careers that you have had. Can you tell us a little bit about your childhood?

RK Well, I think I was kind of really lucky. I was born in the war, and therefore my first memories are about just after the war. There was a kind of euphoria about the liberation, but there was also kind of genuine poverty. And particularly the fact that I experienced poverty, I think, is kind of very crucial in terms of my overall experience and sensibility. Then I was lucky that my parents took me to Indonesia, abruptly, when I was eight. In Indonesia we were also in a euphoric situation because it had been just liberated from the Dutch, and that meant that I was in a post-colonial situation, and had to behave in a post-colonial manner. It taught me to be a minority and what it meant to be a minority. Then later I was really lucky that I was to grow up in the 1960s, when people were not really interested in formal education or university degrees, and they were actually encouraging you to pursue what you wanted. That meant that when I was 18, I could be a journalist and even a kind of filmmaker.

MH How did you decide to become an architect? What was the trigger?

RK When I was 23, a group of architects asked me to give a lecture about film. Then those architects took me to Russia, in 1967, which was then deeply Soviet. A particular kind of architecture had been developed in the early part of the Revolution, which was actually very close to scriptwriting. The architects would really propose radically different ways of living, for instance, not in cities, but you could live in the countryside in a small hut and have a collective kitchen 400 meters away in a forest. I realized that you could interpret architecture as a form of scriptwriting, and then I decided to switch because I thought architecture was more interesting and more substantial.

MH You've completed two iconic projects here, the National Library and the Qatar Foundation headquarters—why did you come to Qatar initially?

RK I came because we got a letter saying that the Qatar government was interested in a group of architects doing a group of buildings. They asked me which part I would be interested in. I said that I was interested in the school for diplomacy, because, above everything else, I'm really interested in politics. Then a while later I got a letter saying we'd like you to do a library and the headquarters of Qatar Foundation, and that was a direct commission. So I had the privilege during the Qatar Foundation headquarters project of meeting your mother and capturing her intentions.

MH I remember when I was with Richard Serra driving from his *East-West/West-East* installation, he told me that, in his opinion, you created the best contemporary architecture building derived from our heritage. He felt that the Qatar Foundation headquarters really resembled a modern souq.

RK Whenever you work in a particular context, you're obviously extremely interested and committed to try to do something that is recognizable for the inhabitants, and that falls within local experience and local taste. But, of course, you also want to maintain your own intentions and your own integrity. I think that with architects like Jean Nouvel, myself, and Pei, you can see in all our buildings in Qatar that, on the one hand, we are inspired by Qatar and, on the other hand, we also maintain our own position. I find that a very interesting tension between the two. I think that I was lucky that the façade of the headquarters, which is kind of perforated by quite small squares, which is kind of multiplied in the interior work and reflections in the glass and the different angles of the glass, actually creates a very decorative bubble or decorative enclosure, which has some of the same effects as Islamic architecture, even without directly referring to it. So, I think it's a partly conscious and partly unconscious process where you try to be appropriate.

MH The National Library is an amazing 21st-century library that you have built at the center of Education City. How did you create this concept with the façades and the interiors?

RK What was interesting is that I was instructed in the very beginning that the library had to stimulate reading. When I thought about it, I saw that in the typical library there's a lot of things that are not particularly stimulating or not particularly attractive. There are compartments, there is a complex catalog, there are usually a number of different stories. Often you are quite remote from the books when you enter. That basically suggested to me that I should try to make a building where you enter without many preliminaries, and that once you enter, you are exposed to the entire richness of the books that surround you. That made it interesting to make a building where you enter in the middle and once you enter you are surrounded by terraces of books. Then there was an additional request that came out of the blue to also create a rare book department. We were able as a major improvisation to excavate this space, almost like archaeology.

MH Beside these two projects, you've also curated several exhibitions in Doha with your partners—recently *Virgil Abloh*, as well as the launch of the Qatar Auto Museum with an installation at the National Museum. I find this concept of having a network of thinkers and collaborators as part of your architectural firm really unique. How did you come up with this notion of a think tank?

RK In a way you could say out of desperation. In the mid-1990s, you had a kind of feeling that culture was accelerating. There was an optimism about the world. The internet was beginning to suggest totally different lifestyles and ways of behaving. So, I felt that with our original training as architects we could not be secure in resting with what we knew, and that we basically had to find a way to constantly refresh and add to our own knowledge. That basically became a reason for the think-tank. With our own think tank, we were genuinely able to create a parallel reality for our office, where in the office you focus on building, but outside in this parallel world, we could focus on literally everything else.

MH Transitioning into your next project in Qatar, which is the Qatar Auto Museum, you told me in our last encounter that this is very exciting for you. Why is that the case when it is, after all, the transformation of an existing building?

RK Two things. I think that as part of a genuine reorientation of architecture and more responsible behavior, any architect really feels the pressure right now in finding ways of transforming architecture rather than building new architecture. If you can transform something, obviously it is by definition more sustainable. But I'm also genuinely excited because I love cars and I love driving. I find cars maybe the most eloquent representatives of particular civilizations or particular moments in civilization. For instance, in the seventies, a French car was absolutely different from an Italian car, which was absolutely different from a German car. Cars are the embodiments, in many ways, of ideas.

MH Next year, in fall 2023, you're going to be opening an exhibition on the countryside in our future vocational school. How will this exhibition be different from the one you curated at the Guggenheim in New York a few years ago?

RK In the Guggenheim we opened in 2020 and it was a moment when basically one believed—and the UN statistics were confirming this—that globally people from the countryside were moving in enormous numbers to the cities. There was a risk that the countryside in a couple of decades would be almost empty. What we hope to do in Qatar is different. It's partly different because the mood about the countryside is completely flipped here, but also partly through Covid. Now, people from the cities are actually moving to the countryside again. What we want to look at, therefore, are more serious issues of food production and global distribution. We'll take Qatar as a center and investigate from there.

MH You are involved with the Qatar Blueprint, which we've been working on now for almost a year. It connects Qatar's urban landscape with its natural habitat and the people. Why do you think this is unique and important for a country the size of Qatar to be thinking in these ways?

RK I'm interested in small countries. Basically, coming from the Netherlands, I've been fascinated by Switzerland and how it maintains a kind of uniqueness, and by Singapore and Qatar. The small scale of a particular piece of territory basically enables you to have a comprehensive idea in terms of what direction it could move or develop, and how the different components could potentially relate to each other. At a small scale, you can, paradoxically, have larger and more coherent ambitions than you can have for a huge country that is simply beyond the reach of a single ambition.

MH As someone who visits us frequently, what, in your opinion, is the most unique experience people coming to Qatar can expect?

RK I was really struck by the unique tone of urban life. It's quiet in a certain way. Of course, now the World Cup adds enormous pressure, but there is a kind of serenity and dignity, and not too strong a presence of commercial elements. What I also have begun to deeply appreciate is how beautiful the landscape is, and how in the landscape there are a number of really unique features that, again, have the virtue of being accessible rather than being very remote. I like the humor, kindness, and the intelligence of the Qatari people. I'm not saying this to flatter, but our experience in terms of being able to communicate through mutual intuition and very direct communication has been remarkable.

CONVERSATIONS

×

SOPHIA AL MARIA

Sophia Al Maria is a Qatari-American artist, writer, and film-maker. Her work spans many disciplines, including drawing, film, and screenwriting for TV. It is united by a preoccupation with the power of storytelling and myth, and in particular with imagining revisionist histories and alternative futures. She has held solo shows at the Whitney Museum of American Art in New York (2016), Tate Britain in London (2019), and Garage in Moscow (2021), among others. In the fall of 2022 she has a major show at Mathaf in Doha.

PODCAST CONVERSATIONS TRANSCRIBED

al-Mayassa bint Hamad bin Khalifa Al-Thani (MH)

with

Sophia Al Maria (SAM)

MH You started off working at Mathaf and also making films with the Doha Film Institute. Can you say a little bit more about your artistic beginnings?

SAM It's interesting to consider where one begins. The moment I can trace art becoming a practice for me is a very boring summer indoors at my family's home in Doha. There was nothing to do and nowhere to go for months, so we went to the school supply store to buy glue, glitter, and the municipal school notebooks with the map of Qatar on. I collaged and drew and dreamed my way into a different life. So I suppose I began by being so bored that making art was a means of survival. Later I went to university in Cairo, where I started making video art on the side. I was studying journalism with hopes of working at Al Jazeera, then shifted into literature because the journalism program was disappointing and very focused on producing attractive news anchors, which was definitely not something I either aspired to or was capable of. I fell in with a lot of artists over the five years I was there, which were formative friendships. My first show was a collectively painted mural cartoon called *We Few* for the Townhouse Gallery. I never thought it was something I could do in any serious capacity until much more recently. I obsessively read and watched everything I could from the public library. I owe my education to libraries and librarians, which ironically is what I ended up doing at Mathaf several years later.

MH I remember you were one of the first filmmakers to whom Robert De Niro awarded a prize during the Doha Tribeca Film Festival partnership. How did that make you feel?

SAM I don't think we ever spoke about that night. But firstly, it made me feel surprised. I didn't know I was up for a prize. And someone called and asked if I was coming. I was still at work in Madinat Khalifa at the old Mathaf villa. So I drove to the MIA, and thank goodness my friend Lana Shamma, who knew what was going on, took me aside and put make-up on me and sent me backstage, because I'd been in the library cataloging books so I was pretty dusty. They told me it was to present something. I went back stage and saw De Niro. Which was a shock. My main memory is that the cups of water were covered with plastic. And that I told him a true but probably slightly disconcerting story about having a poster of him in *Raging Bull* on my wall in Doha as a teenager, and it becoming a big issue in the house to have pictures up on the walls until someone finally took it down and ripped it in half so it wouldn't get possessed by djinn.

MH You also wrote your book, *The Girl Who Fell to Earth*, back in 2012, almost 10 years ago. What inspired you to write that memoir?

SAM To be perfectly honest, I didn't want to write that book. I wanted to write a young adult sci-fi/fantasy called *Qasida*. But when I got an agent, I was told that to get a foot in the door I should write what I had already proven to be good at. I had been publishing small essays in *Bidoun* magazine. So, I wrote a proposal and, much to my cringe, it sold to HarperCollins in 2008. Then I decided I wanted to do it: to write a book for the person I'd been at 13 or 14. I know for a fact that if I had read anything like this when I was a kid, something that wasn't written by and for white kids, I would have felt more possibility in my own future. I wrote it to spare some of the pain for kids who struggle around cultural boundaries and especially shame and guilt around language or body, or at least let them know they aren't alone. It's brought me many younger kindred spirits from all over the world, but especially the Gulf, and it feels like a little family.

MH You juggle between the two worlds of the USA and Qatar. How do you think this influenced the trajectory of your life?

SAM The bifurcation of "home" has majorly influenced my life personally. Unlike the conversations around diaspora, the person whose family and origins are split across continents is a particularly late-20th/early-21st-century story made possible by the speed and relatively low cost of jet travel. I spent very little time in the USA. In the past decade, I have been mainly living in London, and, before that, five years in Cairo, so I feel very much that those two cities raised me and gave me a complete sense of home and community and chosen family that neither Puyallup, WA, nor Doha can offer alone. The feeling of being totally "at home" has evaded me my entire life and that is very much a drive within my creative practice.

MH Can you explain Gulf Futurism?

SAM Gulf Futurism is a term I came up with my friend and collaborator Fatima Al Qadiri many years ago to describe an accelerationist phenomenon we witnessed especially around the turn of the century in the Gulf. There was a National Day animation (I think, or maybe it was Asian Games?) that I remember which involved an astrolabe ricocheting a group of children into the future, and that felt like a potent symbol of what was happening. It's no news that the speed of development is something notable in our region, and I wanted to find ways of talking about it.

MH You installed your work *Scout* at the Gwangju Biennale, in South Korea, and in the *Here There* exhibition of Qatari and Brazilian artists, part of the 2014 Year of Culture program between Qatar and Brazil—can you tell me a little about that work?

SAM That piece will be in the new Mathaf show as well, which I am excited about. It was made in a prop workshop in New Zealand, which Peter Jackson used for the *Hobbit* films. It is a sort of ghostly version of dolos, which are huge cement jacks used to break waves and protect coastal lands. I'm fascinated by big engineering design. The way these objects are sort of useless alone, but when many combine they can literally change the landscape, felt like a beautiful metaphor to use about our future feeling so uncertain. Especially with climate change and rising seas. So these pieces are objects of hope, reclaiming time and space collectively toward a more livable future.

MH We also collaborated on producing a work for the Whitney Museum in New York. What was that about?

SAM *Black Friday* was my first major institutional show, curated by Christopher Lew and produced by Anna Lena Vaney, with the Film House in Doha and supported by yourself and QM. That work was about shopping malls and the psychological effect that their scripted architectural environs has on a person who enters it. You become more susceptible to suggestion. You have to buy something to leave—paying a toll, almost—and there are manipulations within the plans of a mall that affect you, like there are no outward-facing windows and therefore no horizons, so you don't know what time of day it is. The piece is voiced by Sam Neill as a white patriarchal "voice of reason" sermonizing over the entire thing. We recorded an Arabic version of the voiceover recently.

MH You have also been working with Peter Webber on film scripts—how do you organize your creative work to incorporate all of your interests?

SAM I worked with Peter on a feature script, *The Raft of the Medusa*, for Raffaella De Laurentiis. Peter took me on as an apprentice after we met in Qatar and I wrote a sample scene for an IP [intellectual property] he wanted to acquire about the history of a shipwreck off the coast of Senegal in 1818 and the painting by Théodore Géricault, *The Raft of the Medusa*. Raffaella was impressed with what I delivered and gave me my first big break. She said, "Why not have Sophia do a draft?", which I did. That draft got me an agent, which got me more work as a screenwriter, which I've been doing ever since. Screenwriting is a craft in the way art or even writing books aren't. I can write a screenplay for my job, it's muscular, and it's formulaic to an extent, especially if you want to get things made.

MH So would you say that differentiation in artistic disciplines isn't that important today?

SAM I'd say the opposite. Some ideas are painting, some are films, some are poems. It's my feeling that their expression and final form should ultimately be led by ideas. Bringing narrative into art often backfires, then being hyper-concerned with aesthetics or politics or philosophy often shuts film people down.

Also, the audiences are just different. It's a delicate dance and I wish there was less differentiation between the disciplines for the sake of my mental health and not having to pursue two separate careers.

MH You just participated at the 2022 Venice Biennale with a solo presentation at the V&A Pavilion of Applied Arts. How did that come about?

SAM The curator Cecilia Alemani contacted me at the beginning of the pandemic. She was doing remote studio visits with many artists I knew. Then I heard nothing for over a year and was so preoccupied it came as a bit of a surprise in September 2021 that I would do the Pavilion of Applied Arts. I jumped into action and started preparing an idea. The subject matter of *Tiger Strike Red* came very naturally as it seemed to expand on work I had started in *Beast Type Song* (2019) for Tate Britain. Both films are about the ghosts of colonialism, only the recent piece was more specifically British colonialism as we shot entirely in London's V&A museum. Both films are set in London institutions, so there is a similar aesthetic, and the same cast and crew. I always involve the voices of family members in my films. The film opens with my young cousin Sarah learning to read English, then asking her mother why she has to speak in English over an image of a new-born camel I met a few years ago.

MH In your upcoming exhibition at Mathaf, which is called ~~INVISIBLE LABORS~~ *daydream therapy*, what are you trying to communicate?

SAM Something real. Something relatable. Something true. The works are humble gestures from me, but they deal with grand themes. I want to communicate my own relationship to the museum and the place, and to center it around a theme of the power of dreaming and meditating and journaling. Daydreaming is a precious resource for envisioning futures. When we cease to do that, we stop seeing new ways to be. Instead, we grow stagnant with no play or sleep.

MH Having your exhibition at Mathaf, a place at which you started your career, must be exciting...

SAM If it wasn't Mathaf, I don't think I'd be doing this show. It's a rare opportunity to be able to return to the place you came from, especially to the institution you once worked in without ever imagining that one day you'd be an artist too. It was funny seeing the mascot cartoon characters I drew more than a decade ago still sold on buttons and tote bags. I have a different perspective, power dynamic, and relationship to the changed institution. But some things remain the same. Sometimes the team send things from Mathaf's archive asking, "Is this your handwriting?" The things we leave behind, the trail of sticky notes or videos on hard drives, is very much the center of this show. Like the old Arabic poetry trope, *Al-Atlal*. For me it always comes back to that place of quiet reflection. Which I guess, in a way, is just to dream.

CONVERSATIONS

×

MASSIMILIANO GIONI

Massimiliano Gioni is an Italian curator and contemporary art critic based in New York, where he is the Artistic Director at the New Museum. Gioni was the curator of the 55th Venice Biennale in 2013. For Qatar Museums, he curated *Murakami-Ego* by Japanese artist Takashi Murakami in 2012 and the major Jeff Koons exhibition *Lost in America* in 2021.

PODCAST CONVERSATIONS TRANSCRIBED

al-Mayassa bint Hamad bin Khalifa Al-Thani (MH)

with

Massimiliano Gioni (MG)

MH Massimiliano, you're curating your third show for us at Qatar Museums with *Forever Valentino*. Can you tell me about this upcoming fashion exhibition?

MG *Forever Valentino* is an exhibition that looks at the career of Valentino Garavani and tells the story of this maison, which has become truly legendary in Italy and the world. It does so particularly through the perspective of the relationship between Garavani and [creative director] Pierpaolo Piccioli, and the maison and the city of Rome. Rome has been a source of inspiration, and the place where Valentino and the maison are still deeply rooted. We decided to create a kind of instant city, or a pop-up dreamlike city, that unravels in the spaces of the exhibition. The central concept is the idea of the *capriccio*—a tradition of the Italian baroque, it's basically landscapes of the imagination in which different fragments of the city are combined together in an architectural fantasy. So we approach the exhibition as a *capriccio*, or as a collage of different environments that takes the viewer inside the maison headquarters, inside the atelier, where ideas and new pieces of haute couture are developed, and also around fragments of the city of Rome.

MH Incidentally, Valentino just had an haute couture show on the Spanish Steps in Rome. Did you see that?

MG Yeah, we'll bring a version of the Spanish Steps to Doha. You know the old saying that Rome wasn't built in a day? I joke that if there is a place where Rome can be built in a day, it's certainly Doha, and that's what we are attempting to do with this show.

MH It is interesting that you describe the Valentino show as an art exhibition, because art today is pretty much influencing many of the fashion designers, and a lot of museums are making it a priority to showcase fashion exhibitions—to engage the audience with the other art collections.

MG Well, I think it's obviously a dialogue that exploded sometime in the mid-1990s. I think art understood that the speed of fashion and the global outreach of fashion, and the kind of emerging industry that fashion was creating, was very inspiring, both in terms of ideas, but also in terms of economics and sheer scale. Fashion itself has always looked at art for inspiration. I think the case of Takashi Murakami and Louis Vuitton [Murakami's take on the brand's monogram canvas holdall was the It-bag of choice circa 2003] changed the game completely. But if we look back also to the history of art, I think Dadaism, Surrealism, and Futurism all imagined the possibility of reinventing the universe, literally, from the spoon to the city, and within their reinvention, fashion and clothes and the way we present ourselves were very important. Schiaparelli was making work with Salvador Dalí already in the 1920s and 1930s. There is a famous Italian curator and critic whose name is Achille Bonito Oliva who used to say there is a big difference, though, between fashion and art, because fashion dresses humanity, and instead art is meant to reveal humanity, not conceal it.

MH You are an Italian curator, curating one of the biggest Italian brands, Valentino, during the biggest year for Qatar, our World Cup year. But the Italian team hasn't qualified for the tournament. Will art and fashion compensate for the football team's absence?

MG I don't know if it's sad that, you know, this year culture and art fly the flag for Italy more than sports. But, you know, to tell you the truth, as sad as I am, it's been that way for a long time now. We are certainly known more for our art and our culture than for our soccer, and we are glad that we have other things that can get people talking. The irony is that when Italy won the men's UEFA European Championship [in 2020], there was that famous photo of the Italian team looking so stylish and beautiful, and yet this year they could have been here all dressed in Valentino.

MH You curated Takashi Murakami in 2012 and Jeff Koons in 2021 for us. Can you tell us a bit about the experience you had with the first show, and the impact it had in Qatar, and of Koons in 2021?

MG I can say everything changed and nothing changed in the sense that the seeds of what was happening were already there and visible in 2012. For example, this space itself where we did the show in 2012 [Al Riwaq Art Space] was still somewhat raw and Takashi took great advantage of it. He installed almost a circus with a 100m-long painting. Now, 10 years later, the building is a world-class museum that really allows for the most incredible loans and the most incredible, apparently effortless, presentation. But the energy is the same. What also has changed is the tissue and the network of museums in which every work is now placed. Before, the dialogue was really between the Museum of Islamic Art and Al Riwaq and Katara. Now all these institutions are embedded in an incredibly rich context of other museums, from the National Museum, most notably, to the Fire Station. It's an incredible landscape of culture and museums that has grown.

MH We were in Athens together not long ago and I was asked about what they termed "censorship", but we call respecting our culture. What's your view on this, bearing in mind you just curated the Jeff Koons show for us—a very provocative artist?

MG Even in New York nowadays, one needs to be extremely sensitive to content. I mean, just to discuss the recent conversations around the Philip Guston show, you know, whether or not it was appropriate to show the Ku Klux Klan paintings and what would it mean? There is a lot of conversation around sensitivity and the ways in which people react to images. Paradoxically, this is probably more heated in New York, or in America, at the moment than elsewhere. I believe that my role and the role of art is to go to places and to present itself, and, through its presence, stimulate a dialogue and a series of questions. Art is the place where we learn to coexist with different ideas and different values. I think my job is to be with art and to be with art in places that might have different ideas. And those different ideas are at times not comfortable with some expressions of the work of an artist. In my exchanges with you and your institutions in Qatar, I never felt that the decisions were draconian. We were given parameters right at the start. We understood what they were. They did not destroy the possibility of the show, even with such a provocative artist as Jeff Koons.

MH We just installed Pipilotti Rist's *Your Brain to Me, My Brain to You* at the National Museum of Qatar. I remember going around the Pipilotti exhibition at the New Museum a few years ago, and I took my children who never wanted to leave that show. How did you, as a curator, choose her?

MG Pipilotti is incredibly special, super generous, very warm, adventurous. She's the only person I know that went to China during the lockdown and did three weeks in a hotel by herself because she was going to visit a site for a show. She's one of these artists that really goes beyond the borders of art and becomes part of culture in general. The first time I worked with her was actually in Milan. We did a beautiful show with the Fondazione Nicola Trussardi in an abandoned cinema—one giant room with a screen that was 40m wide. Then in New York, we had this incredible show that was one of our most visited ever. It was like a massage of people's brains and eyeballs. Earlier, I said we go to museums to learn to exist and coexist with what we don't understand. And I think another reason we go to museums, it's because it's a kind of dream of the mind and the senses, an awakening of your entire physical experience, and Pipilotti excels in that.

MH You know, we're looking at devoting a Year of Culture to Italy at some point. What would be the best blockbuster show to represent Italy at Al Riwaq?

MG Many great curators before me have attempted kind of histories of Italian art—Germano Celant, sadly, who passed away in 2020, and who curated the KAWS exhibition in Qatar. He did a beautiful show called *The Italian Metamorphosis* at the Guggenheim, which combined design, fashion, and art. Interdisciplinarity is maybe a characteristic of Italian thought, not just of art. And there could be an interesting dialogue across the centuries. I always thought one could tell the history of art in Italy based on gestures. We are famous for gesticulating and speaking with our hands, but if you look at the history of art, it is also a history of gestures and movements, particularly in the 19th-century art. Italy is the country of melodrama and, you know, we have very theatrical gestures.

MH Is there an exhibition you haven't yet curated or dream of curating?

MG I don't know if you had a chance to see a show we did in the Palazzo Reale, Milan, called *The Great Mother*. It's an exhibition where you can move from contemporary art to modern art, where you can combine Surrealism and contemporary art. These kinds of trans-historical shows are what excite me the most. Maybe because they are more complex and more difficult to make. I've been thinking of a show roughly called *New Humans* that will look at a different conception of humanity in the 20th century—moments in which ideas of new types of humans have been developed in science fiction and also in the avant-garde, from the early robots and automata that the Dadaists and the Surrealists conceived to current conversations around artificial intelligence and the limits between the organic and inorganic.

CONVERSATIONS

FATMA IBRAHIM
AL SEHLAWI

Fatma Ibrahim Al Sehlawi is a Qatari architect and beekeeper. She is the co-founder of Atlas Bookstore (2015) and the co-founder of Studio Imara (2017). In parallel, Fatma has been leading the Qatar Blueprint project at the Office of H.E. Chairperson of Qatar Museums.

PODCAST CONVERSATIONS TRANSCRIBED

al-Mayassa bint Hamad bin Khalifa Al-Thani (MH)

with

Fatma Ibrahim Al Sehlawi (FAL)

MH Fatma, can you tell us a little about the work that you are doing with Rem Koolhaas and his team on the Qatar Blueprint?

FAL The Qatar Blueprint is a response to a request by our Amir, His Highness Sheikh Tamim bin Hamad Al Thani, to explore ways in which the different regions across Qatar can be unlocked to enrich the lives of their residents—and also attract visitors, both residents of Qatari and foreign tourists. We're doing this by surveying and cataloging everything that the country has to offer, in terms of its history and its physical and social assets. We're following the structure of the Qatar National Master Plan, which divided Qatar into eight municipal divisions. We are looking to expose a distinctive character for each one. We are confident that the other municipalities of Qatar can be as well-known as Doha if what they have to offer can be better publicized and given narrative shape. For example, Al Shammal with all its heritage sites, farms, and different marine environments is so different in character to the suburban municipality of Um Slal. The differences should be known and celebrated.

The Qatar Blueprint is a think tank, which sits under Your Excellency's office and leadership, with our long-time collaborators Rem Koolhaas and Samir Bantal [the director of AMO, the think tank founded by Rem Koolhaas] helping on conceptual issues, while I'm leading the on-ground research, public consultation, and content generation from our offices here in Doha. The end result will be a visual databank, which we'll make accessible as a comprehensive planning tool to other state and private entities working on development projects. There will also be an exhibition and a book publishing our findings.

MH Why is a planning document of this scope so important?

FAL Qatar has been going through rapid development surges, one following the other. We haven't had the opportunity to slow down and take stock, and document everything the country has to offer in all the various sectors—sports, education, culture, ecology, and so on. The Qatar Blueprint will pull together all this information, for all eight municipalities, in one comprehensive document. This has never been done before.

When it's complete, not only will the Qatar Blueprint be a tool for future planning, but it will also be a record of the current physical state of the country. It's an archival project. This knowledge is going to lead to more efficient planning, such as avoiding unplanned conflicts between projects, and identifying gaps. It will be a positioning tool for the country—which is the main reason we were tasked with this project.

MH We have already executed some of the Blueprint with the zoning and linking heritage villages.

FAL Yes, over the past year, while most of the country has been sprinting towards the World Cup, we've been working in the background, surveying the different municipalities. We've been doing on-site research, interviews, and helicopter rides over Qatar. Every Thursday last winter was dedicated to a tour of a specific municipality, and we've come across incredible discoveries. Remember the hot springs we visited in the South? The prehistoric "dugong cemetery"? The oral history project by the old Qatari women in Al Khor, who also cooked an incredible authentic Qatari brunch for us... Qatar has so many hidden treasures, in terms of physical places, and people. By mapping all the different assets of each municipality, we're now able to find ways to distinguish and link them, and create synergies between them.

MH I remember the first time I saw you was at Art Basel, you were working in Lusail – what did you enjoy about that project?

FAL As a fresh graduate from architecture school, it was incredible to be given the chance to work on a new city and see it come to life. My first project was to design the manhole covers of Lusail City, and when I walk over them now, I feel extremely proud. Another great opportunity was to design and select the plant palette for the city's public areas. Walking along the Lusail Marina waterfront promenade today, seeing the trees I selected now grown into mature plants, gives me so much satisfaction.

And I do remember our first meeting. It was 2011 and I was assigned to collaborate with Qatar Museums and the Herzog & de Meuron teams on the master planning of Al Maha Island, which consisted of the future Lusail Museum, a convention center, a hotel, and a public park at the time. We all traveled to Basel for a design workshop at Herzog & de Meuron's offices and that is where I met you, not knowing it was the start of a long working relationship. Soon after, I joined Qatar Museums, and, to my surprise, my first meeting on my first day was with Your Excellency and Rem Koolhaas; I was assigned to work with him on the masterplan of Media City. This was the start of my involvement in several masterplanning projects with Rem and the Office for Metropolitan Architecture (OMA), leading to the opening of their office in Doha and working on the Qatar Blueprint with you. Looking back, it also was the seeding stage of building Qatar's creative economy.

MH Today the city of Lusail has become a reality. How do you think the forthcoming Lusail Museum and the heritage houses project will add value to the whole neighborhood?

FAL Lusail has delivered on the intentions of its masterplanning team, as an urban extension of Doha northwards. It's a mixed-use smart city, mostly developed by the private sector. Culture, heritage, and art are fundamental pillars of every livable and appealing city. We already have lots of public art installations in Lusail delivered by Qatar Museums, and these have elevated Lusail's identity. I think the addition of the Museum and the activation of Lusail Heritage Village will only strengthen that identity. They will improve the quality of life for the area's inhabitants, increase value for investors, and draw visitors. Lusail Museum will become the neighborhood's cultural beacon, adding a new level of intellectual, cultural, and global content. The Heritage Village will connect the new city to its past, and emphasize its historical relevance and context. Things like this make a city more humane and familiar. The Heritage Village will connect the new city to its past, and give it some historical relevance and context. Things like this make a city more humane and familiar.

MH You worked on the *Making Doha* exhibition with Rem's team—tell me something about that experience.

FAL It was four months before the opening of the National Museum of Qatar when Rem introduced me to Samir Bantal over coffee at the Sharq Hotel— Rem's favorite hotel in Doha. He mentioned that you'd asked him to work on an exhibition about the architecture of Doha to be held at the new museum, and open on the same day as the museum. He knew that I had been researching the evolution of the city's architecture, so he suggested that I work on the exhibition's content. Qatar Museums commissioned Atlas Bookstore to generate the content, and Rem, Samir, and I co-curated the exhibition, which was designed by OMA. It was a great experience because the exhibition allowed me to collaborate with a number of experts, including a filmmaker, an urban photographer, and a historian. The exhibition became a starting point for a national archive of the country's urban development, rich in images, physical models, films, drawings, and, most importantly, interviews with those who contributed to this development. We've talked about finding a permanent space for *Making Doha* as a public display, and a reference for architecture students. I look forward to this happening after the World Cup.

MH You are the founder of the Atlas Bookstore. Can you tell me something about the idea behind this?

FAL I co-founded Atlas Bookstore in 2015 with my sister Reem to share a passion for the architecture and urbanism of West Asia and North Africa. I opened the store in a small project space at the Doha Sheraton Hotel, which is itself a modernist architectural gem from 1982, designed by American architect William Pereira. The bookstore sells books and magazines as well as acting as a reference library. We then welcomed new team members allowing the bookstore to act as a research engine for different projects, such as the *Making Doha* exhibition. Selections of our books traveled to different exhibitions in places such as Kuwait, Bahrain, Dubai Design Days, and the Vitra Design Museum. We've an upcoming participation at VCUarts Qatar's fall exhibition this year. Reem is now growing the collection to include environmental histories and futures of the region. And an upcoming contribution by Atlas will be published in a book titled Doha Modern, which documents a playground project by the artist Shezad Dawood, commissioned by Qatar Museums.

MH You also have Studio Imara, what service does that provide?

FAL Studio Imara was co-founded in 2017, together with Nasser Alemadi, a colleague of mine for many years at Qatar Museums. It started as a side project through which we designed theoretical architectural concepts as a response to the city. A few years later, during the Covid-19 lockdown, we were approached by friends and new clients who wanted us to design their new homes with the living concepts they had developed during the lockdown period. Our new studio is scheduled to open in the coming months. It will share a space with Atlas Bookstore, and we hope to increase our presence on the rapidly growing creative industry scene here in Qatar.

THE POWER OF CULTURE PODCAST

CLOSING THOUGHTS

People often mistakenly believe that the Gulf and Arab countries have a single identity. The reality is that each has its own vision for development. In Qatar, our focus is on cultivating talent by providing access to quality education, healthcare, and sport and cultural experiences, while preserving our Islamic values, Arabic language, and our ancestors' heritage. What you will find here is a modern nation rooted in the authentic experience, be it food, music, language, culture, heritage, fashion, and more—a nation that wants to celebrate its traditions and history with the world, while embracing and tolerating different cultures. Being on ancient trading routes, with many civilizations passing through, Qatar has been open to the world for centuries. We are now ready to welcome you.

Qatar is a metropolis—a place where you can find all nationalities sharing their everyday lives. I had the honor of working closely with my father when many of our organizations were first established. I have learned so much from observing how he relentlessly multitasked, always striving toward the creation of a modern yet traditional country. I have also had the honor of working closely with my brother over the past nine years to position Qatar as a cultural center serving all of humanity. Under the leadership of both my father and brother, I have been motivated and inspired to learn more about our past, and find ways to translate that into a contemporary language that is accessible and understandable to all.

Twelve years ago, during a TED talk, I discussed the notion of globalizing the local and localizing the global. A decade on, I have reflected on what I can share with my community—on the importance of raising children with a global perspective, while ensuring they have a strong local identity. I am hoping that these stories, projects, and programs will inspire you, as they inspired me, to rise to the occasion of being a better human—by being present in a world full of distractions, yet embracing our society and its differences, and being less judgmental and more compassionate toward others. I am hoping the youth of this country, including my children, nieces, and nephews, will be proud ambassadors of what Qatar has established for the future of this region.

On a personal level, my husband and I have always taken our children to see as much art as possible, just as our parents did. They have been to museums in all the cities we have traveled to, visited archaeological and historical sites, and seen every exhibition that we have organized in Qatar. Just as our parents did, we are not only giving our children an education but teaching them about life beyond the walls of school and the limitations of written text. And just as we do with our children, our hope is that every mother, father, teacher, and educator will encourage their children and students to learn about different parts of the world through the experiences of museum visits and cultural exchanges. Investing in our children beyond the classroom is essential to promote a better understanding of the world around them, and by default builds a sense of tolerance and respect.

Another aspect we find equally important and rewarding is for them to engage in making things. To use their hands to create and re-create their own worlds, from painting on canvas to spray painting and tie-dying their own clothes; from making something in the kitchen to building something in the garden, or mixing sound and content on their digital screens—there is no limit to creativity, and we should nurture it. Every child is born an artist, and it is so important to give them the space to play and create their own inner worlds, using simple tools to express themselves. The skills of creative thinking will take them far in life. They will be more connected to themselves, and better problem solvers and mediators in a world that needs them. Allow them to venture outside the paths that societal expectations have created for them, and let them fail, not once, twice or three times, but as many times as they need before they find their calling and embark on their own unique journeys. It is vital to remind ourselves that they too will have their own lives and that the best thing we can do is empower them with the knowledge and skills to be both resilient and human in a complex world. To guide and observe, without the need to judge and control them.

I feel privileged to have been given this responsibility, first by my father, then by my brother, to invest in the people that I love—the people of a country that has given me and the world so much. In compiling the contents of this book, I have revisited memory lane and realized just how much we have accomplished in a very short time. I have no doubt that by the time it is published I will be aware of the many things that have been forgotten. I hope to publish an update every two years, and, in the meantime, support the content and context of our projects through our #QatarCreates digital platform. Each project, commission, and program builds from the past, celebrates the present, and looks to the future. I hope that through these reflections you have been inspired to learn more about our culture, and do more for the preservation of our environment. That you have gained new tools of how to use the museums, collections, exhibitions, creative hubs, and public art to give you a global view of the world. Last but not least, the contents of this compilation of reflections would not have been possible without the dedication of the people working in the various organizations mentioned. I thank each and every one of them, from the bottom to the top of the employment pyramid, from the laborers to the decision makers, for their work and contributions. I look forward to continue curating our futures together; and to realize the Qatar National Vision 2030 and beyond.

al-Mayassa bint Hamad bin Khalifa Al-Thani on a camel as a child.

Cover	Render of the Art Mill Museum by Alejandro Aravena and ELEMENTAL, due to open in 2030.
6	Courtesy of al-Mayassa bint Hamad bin Khalifa Al-Thani
8-9	Original map courtesy of Qatar Tourism
14	Courtesy of National Museum of Qatar
17	Louise Bourgeois, *Maman*, 1999; Qatar Museums © 2022
18-19	David Levene
22	Kamran Jebreili/AP/Shutterstock
25	Jeff Koons, *moon (light pink)*, 1995–2000; Rik Van Lent
30	© FIFA
31	Bouthayna Al Muftah x Aubusson; Stephane Sby Balmy @sbyconnection
37	Maryam Al Homaid and Levi Hammett, *Urban Intervals*; courtesy of the artists
38-39	Richard Serra, *East-West/West-East*, 2014; Qatar Museums © 2022
40	Urs Fischer, *Untitled (Lamp/Bear)*, 2005-06; Iwan Baan, courtesy of Qatar Museums
41	Tom Claassen, *Falcon*, 2021; Qatar Museums © 2022
42-43	Damien Hirst, *The Miraculous Journey*, 2013; Qatar Museums © 2022
44	Rudolf Stingel, *Untitled*, 2016; Qatar Museums © 2022
45	Shouq Almana, *Egal*, 2022; Qatar Museums ©2022
46-47	Faraj Daham, *The Ship*, 2022; Iwan Baan, courtesy of Qatar Museums
48	César Baldaccini, *Le Pouce*; Qatar Museums ©2022
49	Tony Smith, *Smoke*, 1967; Qatar Museums ©2022
51	Simone Fattal, *Gates to the Sea*, 2019; Qatar Museums © 2022
	Isa Genzken, *Rose III*, 2016; Qatar Museums © 2022
	Subodh Gupta, *Gandhi's Three Monkeys*, 2008; Iwan Baan, courtesy of Qatar Museums
	Ghada Al Khater, *A Blessing in Disguise*, 2018; Qatar Museums © 2022
	Louise Bourgeois, *Maman*, 1999; Iwan Baan, courtesy of Qatar Museums
	Mark Handforth, *Turquoise City*, 2021; Iwan Baan, courtesy of Qatar Museums
	Richard Serra, 7, 2011; Iwan Baan, courtesy of Qatar Museums
	Saloua Raouda Choucair, *Bench*, 1969-1971; Iwan Baan, courtesy of Qatar Museums
52	POW! WOW! Festival. Artists shown: Huda Basahal, Myneandyours, RexChouk; Ali Al-Anssari, courtesy of Qatar Museums © 2022
57	Courtesy of the artists and Qatar Museums © 2022
58	Daniel Arsham; Francois Halard, courtesy of Culture Pass Club
60	Qatar Museums © 2022
62-63	Courtesy of Fire Station
64-65	Ai Weiwei: *Laundromat*, © courtesy of Ai Weiwei Studio. Photo © Fire Station, Qatar Museums, 2022
66	Courtesy of M7
67	Courtesy of M7
68-69	Qatar Museums © 2022
70	Courtesy of Philippe Starck
71	Courtesy of QPS Vocational School
72	Getty Images/Craig Barritt
73	Getty Images/John Shearer
77	Courtesy of Museum of Islamic Art
78-79	Logos courtesy of Qatar Museums
82-83	Alamy/Iain Masterton
84	Shutterstock/Mr_Karesuando
85	Courtesy of Museum of Islamic Art
86-87	Getty Images/Peter Adams
89	Courtesy of Museum of Islamic Art
90	Courtesy of Museum of Islamic Art
91	Courtesy of Museum of Islamic Art
92	Courtesy of Museum of Islamic Art
93	Courtesy of Museum of Islamic Art
94	Getty Images/Atlantide Phototravel
95	Courtesy of Museum of Islamic Art
96-97	Richard Serra, *7*, 2011; courtesy of Museum of Islamic Art
100-101	Courtesy of Mathaf: Arab Museum of Modern Art
103	Yan Pei Ming, portraits of Sheikh Hamad bin Khalifa bin Hamad bin Abdullah bin Jassim bin Mohammed Al Thani and Sheikha Moza bint Nasser Al-Missned; Courtesy of Mathaf: Arab Museum of Modern Art

104   M.F. Husain, *Yemen*, 2008;
courtesy of Mathaf: Arab Museum of Modern Art

105   Inji Efflatoun, *Portrait of a Prisoner*, 1960;
courtesy of Mathaf: Arab Museum of Modern Art

106-107 Kader Attia, *Ghost*, 2007;
courtesy of Mathaf: Arab Museum of Modern Art

110-111 Iwan Baan; courtesy of National Museum of Qatar.

112   Sheikh Hassan bin Mohamed bin Ali Al Thani,
Battoulah, 2019; Getty Images/Rubina A Khan

113   Shutterstock/Aldina Abaza

114   Shutterstock/Ben Bryant

115   Shutterstock/Keena Ithar

116-117 Danica O. Kus

118   Courtesy of National Museum of Qatar

119   Courtesy of National Museum of Qatar

121   Courtesy of National Museum of Qatar

122-123 Jean-Michel Othoniel, *Alfa*, 2019;
Qatar Museums © 2022

124-125 Shutterstock/Cristian Zamfir

126-127 Courtesy of National Museum of Qatar

130   Qatar Museums © 2022

132-133 David Levene

135   Photo by Ali Al-Anssari,
courtesy of Qatar Museums © 2022

136   Photo by Ali Al-Anssari,
courtesy of Qatar Museums © 2022

137   Photo by Ali Al-Anssari,
courtesy of Qatar Museums © 2022

138   Photo by Ali Al-Anssari,
courtesy of Qatar Museums © 2022

139   Photo by Ali Al-Anssari,
courtesy of Qatar Museums © 2022

140-141 Photo by Ali Al-Anssari,
courtesy of Qatar Museums © 2022

142-143 Daniel Arsham, *Sports Ball Galaxy*, 2012;
Iwan Baan, courtesy of Qatar Museums

146   ©UNStudio

147   Photo by Ali Al-Anssari,
courtesy of Qatar Museums © 2022

148   © Herzog & de Meuron

149   © Herzog & de Meuron

150   © ELEMENTAL and Qatar Museums

151   James Corner Field Operations;
courtesy of Qatar Museums

155   Courtesy of Mathaf: Arab Museum of Modern Art

156   Taysir Batniji, *Hannoun*, 1972-2009;
courtesy of Taysir Batniji

        Ahmed Mahood, *Iraqi Wedding*, 1987;
courtesy of Museum of Islamic Art

159   © ELEMENTAL and Qatar Museums;
courtesy of National Museum of Qatar

160   Nabil Anani, *Mother's Embrace*, 2013;
courtesy of The Palestinian Museum

166   Courtesy of Qatar Museums

171   Courtesy of Qatar Museums

172   Courtesy of Qatar Museums

179   Courtesy of Qatar Museums

183   Getty Images/Matthew Ashton

189   Brigitte Lacombe

195   Brigitte Lacombe

201   Tosh Basco

207   Brigitte Lacombe

213   Brigitte Lacombe

221   Courtesy of al-Mayassa bint Hamad bin Khalifa Al-Thani

{ACKNOWLEDGMENTS}

Cultureshock would like to thank:

Abdulla Yousuf Al Mulla, Abdullatif Al-Jasmi, Abdulrahman Al-Ishaq, Ahamed Anzel Mashoor, Ahmad Ghazzan Al Masri, Aisha Mubarak Al Sada, Aisha Nasser Al Sowaidi, Alkindi Al Jawabra, Allegra Burnette, Alya Al Khalifa, Amna bint Abdullaziz Al Thani, Amy Wentz, Bouthayna Baltaji, Catriona Collins, Charlotte Cotton, Charlotte Gelmetti, Charlotte Sexton, Charlotte Yeomans, Christian Wacker, Clémence Bergal, Eileen Marie Willis, Elda Kulenovic, Emilia Eyre, Erin Fleming, Essa Ali Al-Mannai, Fahad Ahmed Al Obaidly, Fatema Ali Al Khater, Fatma Hassan Alremaihi, Glenn Adamson, Harry Marlow, Iris Wagner, Janet Johnson, Julia Gonnella, Maha Ghanim Al Sulaiti, Majid Wasi, Manhal Hamadeh, Marisa Bartolucci, Marion Taylor, Maryam Al-Homaid, Massimiliano Gioni, Mercedes Navarro Tito, Mohamad Khundaqji, Mohamad Zaoud, Mohamed El Attar, Mohammed Liyaqat Khan, Mohammed Nasser Al Ansari, Nairouz Fathalli, Nina Geldmann, Olafur Eliasson, Olivia Bouzarif, Percival Castillo, Philippa Polskin, Randa Takieddine, Reem Al-Thani, Rem Koolhaas, Rita Cecilia Bertoni, Rita Varjabedian, Roisin McGuire, Rosanne Somerson, Rouqueya El Karkouri, Saad Iqbal, Sadie Coles, Sarah Foryame Lawler, Sefa Saglam, Sharon Ruebsteck, Sophia Al Maria, Stephanie Cliffe, Tamadur Tariq Al Shamlan, Tania Fares, Thomas Modeen, Tim Marlow, Tom Eccles, Yaser Bishr, Zeina Arida

With special thanks to: Ana Opitz, Fahad Al Thani, Fatma Ibrahim Al Sehlawi and Whitney Robinson

CULTURESHOCK

Project Editor
Andrew Humphreys

Head of Creative
Tess Savina

Production Editor
Claire Sibbick

Editorial Consultants
Caroline Clifton-Mogg
Jane Morris
Alanood Hamad Al Thani

Designer
Tom Carlile

Picture Researcher
Clare Pennington

Production Manager
Nicola Vanstone

Copy-Editors
Ian Massey
Emily Sharpe

Managing Director
Patrick Kelly

Publisher and CEO
Phil Allison

Translation
Wordminds

Printer
Pureprint, UK

2x4

Executive Creative Director
Michael Rock

Creative Director
Sung Joong Kim

Senior Designer
Ben Fehrman-Lee

Director of Client Engagement
Amanda Al-Mahdi

Project Coordinator
Lona Manik